EDUCATION
OF A FALCON

A TRUE STORY OF
ROMANCE AND
ADVENTURE

HOME SCHOOLING WHILE
CIRCUMNAVIGATING THE WORLD
UNDER SAIL

Mike Riley

PUBLISHED AND PRINTED BY MIKE RILEY
ABOARD THE KETCH BEAU SOLEIL
WHILE SAILING THE WORLD

sailingbooks@rocketmail.com

PHOTOS BY MIKE AND KAREN RILEY

ISBN 978-0-9828247-0-2

TABLE OF CONTENTS

Dedication

This book is dedicated to my parents who always wanted me to write, and to Karen and Falcon who put up with my hogging the computer.

Acknowledgements

This book would not have been possible without the helpful members of the FSG world wide and especially to the crews of the boats: Angelica, Aquilla, Cannibal, Cap'n and Kidd, Catania, Caymanifique, Chandelle, Destiny, Deusa, Deus Regit II, El Golea, Endurance II, Erasmus, Ethereal, Gumboot, Jump up, Lyric, My Lou, Nalu IV, Nemir, Nimanoa, Pipe Dream, Sarah, Sea Quest, Shady Lady, Sooke, Symbio, Tropic Moon, Watchfire, Waxwing, Wind Song, Yemanja II, and Yawarra. If I left anyone out it can only be because of that evil drink, rum, you all forced me to drink, which dissolved what is left of my brain!

Foreword

Wh‍en I was a little girl I used to dream of being whisked away by a handsome knight on a white charger to his castle on the hill in some far off land of enchantment. Little did I know that it was going to happen to me. The only difference was the white charger was a red, white and blue sailboat, the handsome knight, a scruffy sailor in blue jeans, and the land of enchantment the many foreign ports of call that charmed and excited my soul. My scruffy sailor acted like a knight in his pursuit of me. He swept me off my feet and made me fall head over heels in love with him. This is the true story of our three way love affair, Mike, Falcon and I, how it started and how it continues to this day.

As I start my third circumnavigation I look back and remember the many 'boat kids', children home schooled while sailing. They all have three things in common. They are very polite, they all can hold their own in adult conversation, and they all excel, one way or the other, when they return to society.

As a professional teacher, with experience in many different countries, I found home schooling incredibly challenging. At first I was at a loss till we developed the techniques Mike describes throughout this book. Learning is much more than the three r's. I knew what age a child should master a certain skill and if Falcon didn't measure up, I became disillusioned and questioned my abilities. Little did I realize Falcon was learning, in his way, at his tempo. In time I used less of my classroom teaching skills, less of the professional teacher and worked with my child one on one. We were a team; a mom and child or a dad and son. It was an all day classroom. It was a very rewarding experience. Any loving parent can do the same, for there is a teacher in all of us.

It may seem unbelievable to others to live the life related in this book. To me it seems unbelievable you can live in a city or on a farm for your whole life. We aren't any different than you. As Mike always says, he is just a regular guy with a streak of stubbornness. He used to be much more aggressive. How he lost that aggressiveness, thank goodness, is related in the book.

This is not a fairy tale. This is the way it happened. It can happen to you, too. The first step of a voyaging life is untying the lines.

Karen Riley
Aboard Beau Soleil
Haiti, 2007

Finding Love While Sailing the World

INTRODUCTION

Extreme fishing was a stupid idea, a really bad, really stupid idea. It started with such clarity, such brilliance, as we sat around the campfire under the coconut palms, that we all looked at each other and said this is the most inventive, fantastic idea ever thought of by the human mind. It is right up there with the invention of the wheel. That is what we said, yeah, we were idiots; I admit it. If one of us men had thought it up, maybe we would have all laughed and gone out and done something sane like juggling nitroglycerin. But, my 12 year old son, Falcon, the pride of the island, devised it and we, as father and male role models, wanted to encourage, or mold, or train him. You know, some guy stuff we made up. Whatever we wanted to do; it was not to offer one of our own up to a shark attack.

We were anchored off Bodrum, an island in the Chagos Group, a very small island in the middle of the Indian Ocean. An island abandoned by world geo-political treaties that forced its inhabitants to relocate to Mauritius, to leave homes, farms, lives for the betterment of a faraway Britain, cold and distant, all to rent one of its distant sisters, Diego Garcia, to America for a military base. The cry 'No Nukes in Chagos' would never disturb the nesting birds in its trees or the turtles laying eggs on its beaches.

We, on the other hand, had atolls full of islands to play with; lagoons full of fish for us to catch if we could, coconuts, limes, breadfruit abounded on abandoned farms. There were no rules except don't sleep on the islands, don't act like a resident, other than that have fun playing Robinson Crusoe. What a totally fabulous life!

The fishing was first rate. Chagos had never been fished commercially and the inhabitants had been off the islands for decades. The lagoon had tons of fish, enough to feed us forever but like always in Eden, the serpent raised its hoary head and we decided to try for bigger fish. We were intelligent enough not to go diving outside the reef where the tigers and great whites held sway. No, we were smarter than that, a little.

Falcon's extreme fishing idea was not to go outside the reef but to fish in the deep holes that were too deep to free dive; we would bring a hand line with a baited hook. We would drop the weighted line and swim around the surface with our fins and masks on, playing the line till we placed it in front of one of the likely caves 100 feet below. The water clarity exceeded 300 feet in this part of the Indian, so it was a little like a video game. We felt distant and separate from the action as we swam around on the surface. The first time we tried it, we came back with a decent coral trout, 10 pounds, big enough to be worthy not so big to have ciguatera.

The next time we went out into deeper water at the entrance but still inside the lagoon looking for bigger fish. Falcon hooked a nice grouper and was fighting it when a tiger, slumming in shallow water, took notice. It wasn't big for a tiger shark, 12 to 13 feet but its behavior set it in a different class. Attracted by the fighting fish, it came in on the bottom in attack mode. Gill slits flaring, back hunched, there was little doubt it was ready to kill. His skin was black and as we watched the tiger's characteristic stripes began to appear vertically along its sides. Falcon resigned himself to the loss of his fishing gear and grouper. The shark saw the fishing line as it approached the struggling fish and immediately changed directions. It ignored the wounded, bleeding, frantic fish, and swam up the line right at Falcon at full speed. Falcon back peddled, still fighting his grouper. Within seconds the tiger was on my son and he was hitting the shark on the nose with his fins as he continued to retreat, swimming on his back, still pulling in his grouper. The shark had his eyes covered with its opaque white lids to protect them while attacking, and its mouth, filled with evil-looking white teeth, gaped wide open as it tried to eat my son. Its tiger stripes were flashing with swiftly changing colors as it attacked. The four of us adults raced in almost without thought. My wife and I screamed in our snorkels to distract the shark, our two buddies from different boats raced in equally determined despite their lack of familiarity with sharks; counter attack from four different directions was too much for the tiger and he turned and sped off after an evil look at me.

Later, when I had time to play, what if, my blood turned to ice as I saw my son in my mind's eye, half eaten in the middle of nowhere, dying in my arms; pieces of him laying around me. The courage of our two cruising buddies, who looked on Falcon as somewhere between a mascot and a junior tribe member, saved his life. As did my 5' 5" wife who, while familiar with sharks, never had to stare down the dead eyes of a tiger before. That night, sleep was impossible and I remembered again how it all started. It was far better for my mental health to think about the far past, than the events of the last 12 hours.

Falcon in Chagos

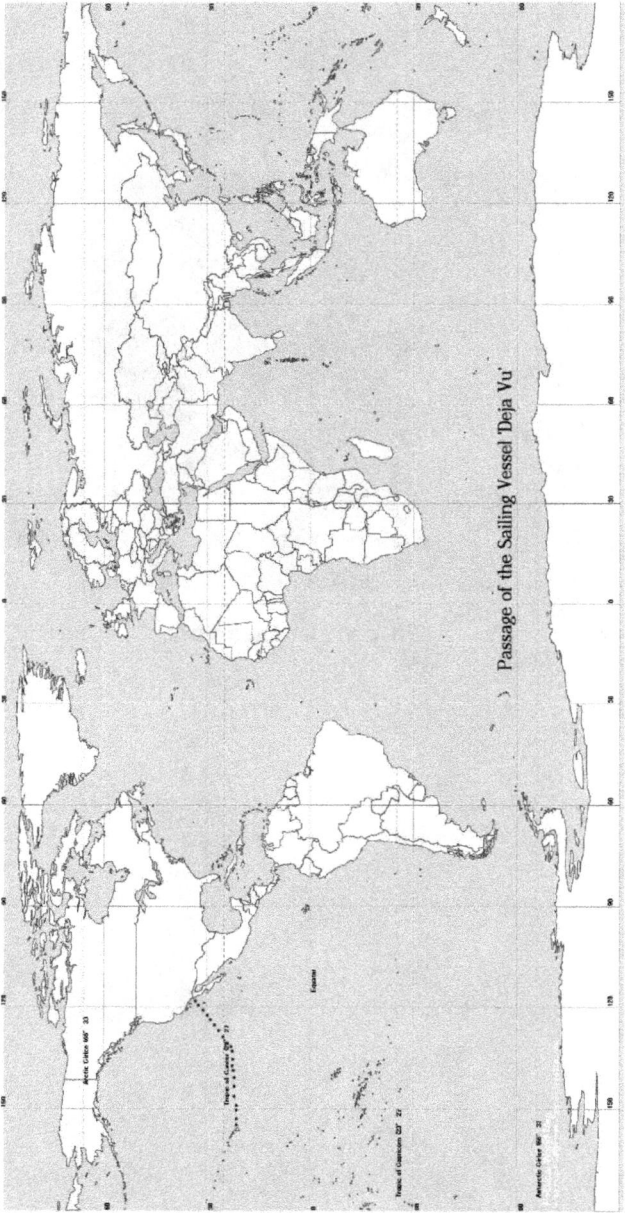

Passage of the Sailing Vessel 'Deja Vu'

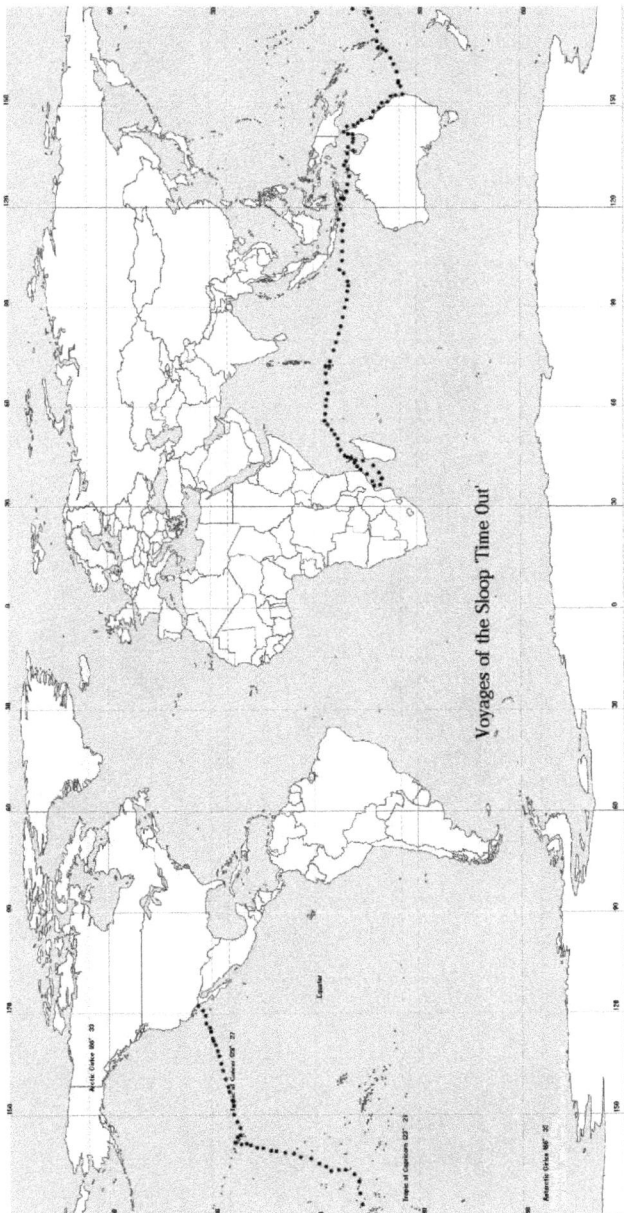

Voyages of the Sloop 'Time Out'

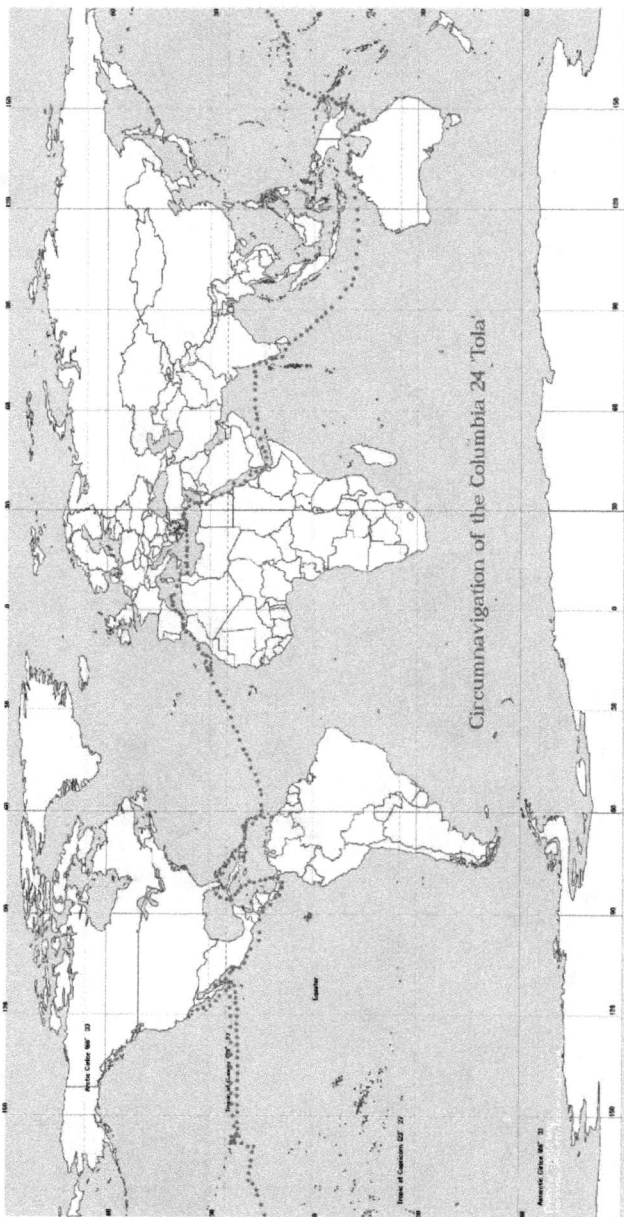

Circumnavigation of the Columbia 24 'Tola'

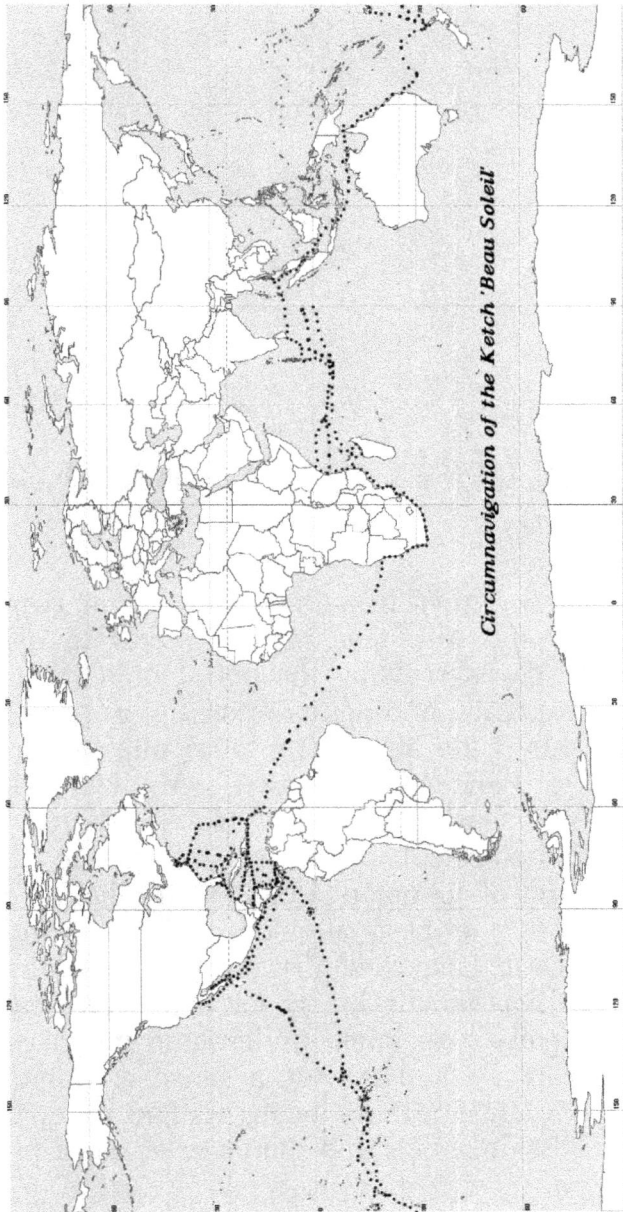

Circumnavigation of the Ketch 'Beau Soleil'

15

FALCON GETS STARTED

I met Karen, my future bride, in the wilds of Papua New Guinea where she was teaching at a private expatriate grade school. I was cruising through, bound from Hawaii and towards Australia and points west, and in need of some place to hide until the dangerous hurricane season in the Western South Pacific had passed. My last crew had become violently seasick in an unseasonal gale ten degrees above the equator and had jumped ship on the American nerve gas island of Johnston Atoll, leaving me, a reluctant single-hander at the best, all alone. Even with all the allures of Rabaul, East New Britain, queen of the South Pacific ports, I was feeling lonely for more civilized female company, company who might understand my jokes. They say girls are always suckers for a sense of humor and I guess they are right but these local girls had never seen TV, or a McDonalds, or a bus that didn't have more pigs than people! Joking with them was damn hard work and resulted more often in blank stares than giggles.

I never was much of a single-hander sailor; I had made many voyages alone, mostly because I couldn't find anyone whom I would enjoy being locked up with in a 24-foot coffin. Wait, let me rephrase that!

To me, sailing was the ultimate freedom. I did what I wanted, when I wanted and however I wanted. If to pay for my freedom required living on a 24-foot boat then that was a very small price to pay, indeed. I often got into trouble either through ignorance or pigheaded stubbornness but at least it was my decision to do it that way not an order from an arbitrary boss or politician. My costs were minimal. One month of working would set me up for the whole year. In those days the last thing that would have ever entered my mind was getting married and having a child. That would just complicate things. Plus I would have to work way more than one month.

It wasn't like I wasn't dating. My social calendar was filled with the immortal pagan song of the South Seas sailor, The Search for the
Wild Wahine.' And the girls of Rabaul were definitely wild enough to keep any sailor occupied for months.

A visa was required before one entered New Guinea, a fact that became apparent to me for the first time as I was clearing customs. The law required them to give me 72 hours and then throw me out. However in my case, as I was a single-hander, they 'managed' to lose my passport and told me that I would have to stay until they found it! They were hoping I would fall in love with a local girl, take her back to America and then she would send for her relatives to come and live in America, the home of 'Cargo'. When I finally did want to leave 6 months later they, all of a sudden, found my passport under the commandant's desk holding up a short leg! Do I sound like I am recommending the single-handed life? I'm not. It is a sad lonely life, filled

17

with challenges but also filled with a decided lack of any one to share your successes with. However, I am getting away from Falcon's story.

Rabaul harbor was the circular caldera of a sunken extinct volcano and was surrounded by seven active volcanoes, any three of which were smoking at any one time. The thing was, that the government had set up a threat warning system that told you how many days you had before you must evacuate because of an eminent eruption. While I was there this was always between one to three days. One to three days to pack up all of the possessions you could carry, get on an airplane or a boat and kiss your job and recent life good-bye. As a result, the expatriates, mostly Australians and Kiwis, who chose to work there, were of a carefree nature and were committed to the grasshopper way of life- have fun now, laugh at the ants and if there ever was winter in the tropics, it could take care of itself. After all, sooner or later, Mon, the volcano, she going a blow. As for the local girls, they never heard of the free love grasshopper era of the sixties. They didn't have to, they invented it 10,000 years ago and have been perfecting it ever since.

New Guinea had just discovered extensive gold deposits the year before I arrived and the economy was flying high. The Kina was worth more than the American Dollar and was the last currency in the world to be truly gold backed. Bring a hundred Kina to the bank and you could walk out with a little gold bar. Unfortunately there was nothing to spend your money on. The company you were working for supplied your housing along with a cleaning girl. A dollar a day extra got you a cooking girl. The market was fabulous. The biggest, most delicious avocado you ever saw cost five cents, a pound of filet mignon a dollar. The beer came in quart bottles and sold at bars for fifty cents. My month of earnings lasted a long time in a place like this! The only two things in Rabaul that were popular to spend your money on were scuba diving and sailing. And I had a boat!

She wasn't a big boat. She was a Columbia 24 that I had modified by cutting the cabin top off and reglassing it back together 14 inches lower, to reduce top hamper, and then extended the cabin 2 feet into the cockpit both to reduce the amount of water the cockpit could hold, in case of a knock down, and add to the living space. I sailed her engineless as the boat wasn't big enough to hold enough fuel to do any good at sea. Engineless, the boat was handy enough to sail into any port and as for calms and doldrums; drop the sails and wait. I named her TOLA, an anagram for Time Out Lives Again. Time Out was a close sister ship, a Columbia Challenger, also 24 feet and engineless, that I had somehow sailed, west about, from San Diego to Africa before I managed to collide with a freighter and smashed up the bow.

It happened in the Mozambique Channel while I was banging down the coast towards South Africa. It was blowing 25 to 30 knots and the seas were easily over 30 feet as I was in the powerful Agulhas current with a contrary wind. This made it very difficult to take any accurate navigational sights, Mozambique was in the middle of its 20 year war, and it was certain death for an American to land. We were coming up to the Zambezi River entrance, which had at times huge islands of grass and trees that swept out to sea, not a good thing to run into on a dark and stormy night. Not knowing exactly where we were, when we spotted a coastal cruiser I foolishly decided to try to speak to him.

It was really great fun to start with. Time Out was a fine sailor and I circled around and around the freighter as we shouted back and forth; me in English, him in Portuguese, my crew in French. One of his men threw out a line and stupidly I tied it onto the bow cleat that was under the dinghy. As we continued to try to communicate an extra large swell pushed us apart, the bowline stretched to almost the breaking limit and then pulled us together like a rubber band. I tried untying the line but it was too tight and as I looked up, there was his hull on top of a swell plunging down upon poor Time Out down in the trough.

It is a miracle that the head stay didn't break instantly. It lasted the half-second I needed to throw my sorry self back to the mast. I got my knife out and cut the line still holding me to the freighter and stared at what was left of my bow. The pulpit had vanished. The first foot of the bow was gone and the poor head stay, that had held on long enough to save my idiotic life, was dangling merrily from the top of the mast with a couple inches of boat still attached. When I had bought the boat, she had single lowers shrouds. I added a baby stay forward to take the place of the missing forward lowers. I am sure that this baby stay saved the mast.

I patched her back together with a lot of duck tape and a few odd pieces of wood and fiberglass and in a daze turned down wind. There was no hope of heading up wind to South Africa. Without a jib she could not point against those seas.

After sailing 500 miles back to Mayotte, the closest civilization down wind in that part of East Africa, and in shock, I sold her to four French Legionaries and flew back to California still in a daze. After a year of feeling regrets for not rebuilding my brave little boat, I bought Tola and set out to try again. More out of stubbornness than intelligence I again decided to sail the boat engineless, to rely only on the sails, to be, as they say, a purist. The boat came with a handy 6 HP outboard that I traded for a good rowing inflatable dinghy. Did I ever regret that trade? Oh, yeah! Only saints are purists and I have walked too often on the dark side to meet the entrance requirements.

I spent 2 years in Mexico and one in Hawaii working on the boat, turning a day sailor into a vessel that could safely cross oceans. It is easy to say that Tola was a Columbia 24 but in reality she was so modified that few could recognize her. Irregardless, I pledged to myself that this boat would make it around the globe.

Anyway, back to Rabaul. I met Karen during a yacht race. This wasn't your average club race. This was Rabaul after all and everything was done to extremes. We were to race out to a rich dude's beach house where he would wine and dine us in luxury. He put up 300 Kina in prize money to the winner. Well! The competition was such that it would take a fluke to win. It was first to finish, no handicap. And the local boats, Farrs, Petersons and multihulls, were not going to let an outsider get their Kina! But hey, there was always the outside chance for an outsider!

I had met an Australian fourth grader on the dinghy dock who was an avid fisherman. It was totally logical to a 9 year old that if the fish were big off the dock, then they would be even bigger if one had a small boat to row out deeper. He made it his life's work to bug me till I let him use my rowing dinghy. I made him jump through hoops before he was allowed to use it in the hopes of discouraging him. Who wanted pieces of bait and dead fish scales all over one's dinghy? But everything I demanded, Matthew accomplished. Whether it was swimming 100 meters, or tying 5 different knots one handed and blindfolded, or cleaning the dinghy with a scrubbing pad every day; he charged forward with a smile and a cheerful attitude. His parents were as interesting. His father was the coach at the local high school. Part of his duties was to escort the girl's volleyball team once a month to the mainland on a barge, a three day voyage! His mother was the Secretary of the yacht club and fruitlessly but continually tried to get me to be the collector of yacht fees. I had many interesting nights at their house relating our various tales.

So it seemed logical when the yacht race came up to enlist the whole family as crew. It was the least I could do to pay them back or forward or whatever. Anyway, we were tied up at the club dock loading up with food and drink, when this sexy, brown eyed brunette in a tight denim skirt and a well filled blouse with the top button undone waltzed down the dock and called out,

"Who needs crew?"

Now, Dear Reader and Fellow Adventurer, you can imagine the thoughts that raced through my brain. Sexy girl, liquor, over night on the beach! This was a night for the 'search for the wild wahine' if there ever was one!

Instantly my hand went up, but so did Margaret's and John's on a slow British 32 footer. The girl picked the wrong boat! She escaped. Damn, foiled again – but we were bound for the same beach! AH-HA!

Well, I soon found out that the escaped wahine was Matthew's fourth grade teacher, Karen Jakos, born in Connecticut and a dual citizen of New Zealand. She was unmarried and on the rebound from a relationship gone bad. She had sailed dinghies and spent two months as crew on a local fishing research ship and didn't get seasick. What
more was there to know? I found out that it was very useful to have a fourth grader as a spy!

So I 'bought' her a beer and gave her my best line with my finest smile. She ended up locking herself in a bedroom for the night! I guess not every girl was a wild one. It seemed my luck was running out. But the two of us did have a grand time dancing on the beach.

Later, back in Rabaul, the social scene continued. It consisted of a different party at a different club every night. Hey, it was better to be social than to sit at home and watch the volcanoes smoke! Two nights after the race, I was at a club that was showing a movie. The projector looked like one that the teachers used when I was in first grade. No one could get it to work. After a half-hour of struggle, Karen walked up and, I am not exaggerating, had it running within 15 seconds. I stared at her willing her to come over and sit next to me. I mean a girl who sailed, who fixed things, who was as sexy as hell, was single, was white and was sitting not 10 feet away from me. Karen however continued to ignore me. What was it with this girl?

I found out from Matthew where her classroom was and made a point of walking by it every day on the way to the market. I started leaving little presents at the office for her. No name, just signed, 'Your admirer.' Ha, I could fight fire with napalm! Every time I walked by, Matthew had all of Karen's students rush over to the window and call out,

"Miss, Miss Jakos, your boyfriend is outside!" Not five days later, she was making her first meal aboard 'Tola.' But to hear Karen tell it, it was all my fault.

It all started the day before when she came on board for a look see. I was showing her all the bells and whistles including the bilge where she managed to locate a bottle of '409' hidden in a back corner where I had forgotten about it. Instantly she went all girlie. Apparently it was the first bottle of her favorite cleaner she had seen in 5 years. This girl had a bad case of homesickness. Suddenly Tola was the reservoir of all things American, whether it was cleansers or magazines or ketchup. We arranged to have dinner on board the following night and she was going to cook. She made lentil burgers at her home, a recipe she had been experimenting with. They were so dry. A starving man would have turned up his nose but not a man in lust. Karen blamed the dryness on my lack of ketchup which she expected to find on board. I artfully agreed that it was entirely my fault and by sacrificing myself on the altar of love I received my reward. They didn't even taste all that bad if you looked at Karen while eating them!

Within a couple of days, we hiked into one of the volcanic craters around Rabaul. Sulfur gas was flowing from yawning crevices everywhere. The jagged rock was warm to the point of almost being too hot. Low rumbling sounds reverberated through my feet and ears. Small tremors rumbled around the crater. Holding hands led to kissing which led to this and that, but I was looking around distracted the whole time, watching out for red hot lava! My first impressions were right. I had my hands on a tiger of a wild wahine!

Hurricane season was drawing to a close and I was thinking of moving on to Australia. I had met this nice Flemish girl who was the captain of the Belgium National Sailing Team. I invited her, Karen and another girl to go sailing. Each girl had to steer, reef and winch around the old central basalt cone sticking 100 feet straight out of the middle of the harbor. Karen won hands down mostly because the Flemish girl stepped on my solar panels, Karen laughed harder at my feeble jokes, and Karen was like, way cuter. Two weeks later, we sailed off thru the islands and the Coral Sea bound towards Cairns, Queensland.

The first night we ran out of wind but managed to ghost into what seemed a comfortable roadstead off New Ireland. Two hours later the tide changed, a swell worked its way in, and we were rolling gunnel to gunnel. It was an unbelievable night, pure hell. But in the middle of it all Karen cooked up a three course dinner on a one burner stove! My god. Did I hit the jackpot or what! The next stop was Irish Cove on the bottom of New Ireland. It was a beautiful spot with a white sand beach, a waterfall between a couple of low grassy hills and a little stream where Karen did laundry and then to rinse, she put a rock on a corner of each sheet and let the stream do the work.

A young boy paddled his outrigger into 'our' bay and asked if we wanted to buy some lobsters. He had one live and one dead one.

"Sure I'll take the live one."

"No, Massa. You must take both," and mentioned a very high price. I assumed that this was bargaining as usual and got into it. I ended up with both and stupidly threw the dead lobster away in front of the boy as I felt I had paid a bit too much.

The next morning as we were in the channel exiting the bay, a flotilla of war canoes was entering. In the first and biggest canoe was our lobster salesman sitting right next to a huge warlike chief who looked just like him. We were in big trouble. The wind was on our quarter which was Tola's best point of sail but the canoes were making a good 4 knots with all of their oarsmen. I had Karen hand me out my machete and sharpening stone, then with one foot steering, I sharpened the machete while staring at the canoes with my harshest captain look. Inside I was quaking in my boots, or would have been if I were wearing any. I glanced at Karen, down below, with a look of loss and sorrow.

"Keep your head down no matter what happens," I whispered to her. I headed straight at the chief's canoe and asked myself, 'Where is my engine when I need it?' The heartache of dying so soon after finding true love threatened to crack through my stony façade. With a start I realized what I had just thought. Was it really true love after all these years and who knows how many women? Or was it just the tension of the moment?

We squeezed past the last section of reef where I could bear off just when they came within spear range. I maintained my stony look while praying on the inside as the first flight of spears was launched.

"I love you, Karen," I whispered to myself. The god of the Papua New Guinea tribes must have been looking the other way as a wave rocked the canoe just as they threw their spears and they all landed short by a few inches scratching the paint on the side of my hull. Before they could launch another volley we were out of range and heading for the safety of the deep blue sea. Tola was a great sailor and once she had the wind just forward of her beam I let her have her way. I let her fly and fly and fly far farther than any canoe could ever hope to catch us. I was much kinder than usual to Karen the rest of that day and stood most of her watches that night. The fear was still coursing through my veins and I couldn't sleep. And a question was burning in my soul.

Two days later, we were 4 degrees south of the line and in the middle of a baby hurricane. Even though the storm was in the growing stage and was only blowing 30 knots, it was raining like hell and was totally miserable. I had closed Karen down below out of the rain and then in the midst of a particularly evil gust, I heard a persistent knocking on the companionway doors. I slid open the hatch a crack and Karen asked,

"Can I come outside?"

"You don't have any rain gear or foulies, Karen. You will get totally soaked."

"I do so have a rain coat," came the emphatic reply! She held up a little plastic bag, the kind that has a flimsy fake plastic coat squished inside and the whole thing fits in to a pocket. Her eyes were pleading so hard and their color looked so fetching in the sheet lightning that just I couldn't say no. Her 'raincoat' lasted all of 5 seconds till it was torn off her and carried up into the low flying clouds. Somehow she sneaked into my foul weather jacket and we shared it for two more hours till we anchored in the lee of a high tropical isle just as the low was leaving our area.

It was a great anchorage, very well protected from the wind and most of the rain fell on the island. Already anchored, was a New Zealand ketch with two ten year old twins on board. We stopped, as cruisers do, and talked about the weather and told tales of our adventures. They had been out 3 years and were home schooling their children.   New Zealand, being a fairly rural country, encouraged home schooling and supplied the books and materials free to its citizens.   The kids seemed very well adjusted and were easy to talk to.   A little warning bell went off in my head.   Karen seemed much too interested in the kids.   But the rum came out and I was silly enough to forget all about the bell.

Three days later the weather was great but the next group of islands only anchorage was over a hundred feet deep and the light was fading.   The reefs of New Guinea were no place to sail at night.   We hadn't made the distance I was hoping for, as the wind had been light all day.   I dropped my best CQR, with a variety of jib sheets tied to the bitter end of the rode in a likely spot and hoped that it would hold for the night.   No worries, Mate, it held, but the next morning the anchor was well and truly stuck in coral far below.   We tried for hours to free her but to no avail and there was no way I could free dive that deep.   And there was also no way I was going to leave without my best anchor.   Karen started praying to herself quietly. For my part, looking
at my knotted anchor line I wondered if I was really willing to tie the knot at my advanced age of thirty seven.

The tide was low, so I tied the rode as tight as I could.   As the tide came in and the bow went lower and lower into the water and the stern came out, Karen's prayers became higher and shriller.   I decided the time had come for the ultimate sacrifice.   I laid the spinnaker pole across the foredeck and took Karen by the hand.   We were about to get married!

"Jump across this spinnaker pole with me and you jump into a life of joy and adventure, of happiness spiced with strife.   Jump with me and we'll be on a honeymoon the rest of our life.   Jump with me, you lovely, lovely lass, jump and become my wife!"

To her credit, Karen never hesitated. She may have thought that it was all a lark, not knowing how I had avoided marriage all these years, but eyes shining, we jumped together. Of course, it was probably our weight surging forward, but at the moment we landed, the anchor broke loose. How we laughed at the goodness of life. How silly we were. If only we knew then what the future held.

We stopped at the Goodenough Islands which had an actual village instead of a hut here and there. It was really nice. We were shown where we could bathe in the stream, a spot for couples, far away from the men section and even further from the woman's area. Karen was suffering from some arthritis in her hands and negotiated with a local girl to do her laundry for some rice. The girl did an outstanding job and Karen gave her a pound of rice. It was too much apparently as the next day she was back with a little handmade doll. Karen gave her a necklace. The next day she was back again and after this trade, Karen used sign language and what pidgin she knew to say that this was enough. It was easy to see why this was such a nice village, everyone else had all your stuff and you had theirs! It was a beautiful island. It was so clean. Each house was surrounded by giant clam shells that the family members filled every day with sea water. After it evaporated the cook only had to go to the nearest shell to get some salt. As we walked around, the toddy collectors lowered bamboo flasks down to us from the tops of the trees to give us a taste.

The Coral Sea was kind to us. Queensland and the Great Barrier Reef were a delight; and six months later, we were married properly on our foredeck by the Catholic priest who was also the port minister of Gove in the Northern Territories of Australia. We rafted up with two big boats to hold all the people for the party and ceremony. Everyone kept tying their dinghies to our stern as they arrived as it is an Australian superstition that you will have as many children as there are dinghies tied to your boat for the ceremony. I kept moving their dinghies over to the other boats every chance I had, leaving just our own little 'Rascal', as I wanted to make a quick getaway after the party. Little did I know that the superstition would be true for us. It was a great wedding. I bought 20 cases of beer and the 40 of us managed to drink it all!

We had a great time on the start of our honeymoon. We spent it sailing across the top of Australia, one of the last truly wild spots left in the world. One anchorage we shared with a witch doctor. We left him some food by his cave in the hopes for good luck! In another we snuck up on some wild cattle just for a lark. Only later did we find out they were giant Asian Buffaloes, one of the most dangerous animals alive. They were a member of the big five, the animals that when shot, attack. The Wessel group was fabulous. It was so virgin that as we walked along the beach 5 foot long fish swam up to us in a foot of water as if they had never seen a walking tree, and definitely never a man before.

Darwin was Darwin, fair shopping, great beer. A week set us right, and we were off across the big Indian Ocean! Two weeks later we were in Ashmore Reef. Ashmore was a great place. It consisted of ten rather small sand bars on top of a few reefs. No palm trees and no hotels. It was known mostly for being where nautilus shells go to die. It was on our way to Christmas Island, so why not stop?

People! We thought we would have the place to ourselves for a Blue Lagoon chapter in the continuation of our honeymoon, but it was not to be, at least not alone.

We found two Aussies who were trying to kill each other. With knifes. Really. They worked for the Oil Companies, and gave radio direction signals to the oil rigs to enable them to position themselves correctly. This was during the time that GPS was just starting to launch satellites and Sat Nav was not accurate enough for drilling. Their tour of duty was six months, six months in Darwin, six months out there by themselves. As there was nothing else to do they both turned to shell collecting. And beautiful shells there were, rare enough so that any museum would drool over them!

When we arrived the radio operator was accusing the other bloke, the cook, of stealing his best shells. The cook denied it and said his best shells were missing also but he wasn't going to point fingers.

We had one bottle of wine left from Cairns where we bought a couple of cases of Cab Sav for a dollar a bottle. Remember, working one month a year means you drink your share of rot gut! Anyway, we offered to share the bottle with the two of them if they would only cool down and sit together in the same tent and talk to each other. As luck would have it, the wine had half turned to vinegar; but we drank it anyway!

While I was trying to keep the conversation neutral, non confrontational and non lethal, Karen said,

"I know who the thief is." You could have heard a pin drop, if a pin would make a sound dropped on a raked sand floor.

"And there he is!" And with a dramatic motion she pointed to the leg of a table across the hut. We rushed over and there was a hermit crab just reaching the top of the table. He strolled thru the collected shells till he found one he liked, an Emperor of the Seas, worth perhaps a thousand dollars, and before our unbelieving eyes he switched homes and started back down the leg of the table!

Perhaps it was the vinegar wine but we rolled on the sand laughing so hard we had to hold our stomachs for the pain.

What a feast that night! We ate like kings! As long as kings eat out of cans accompanied with nautilus meat! It was with a sad heart when we left a week later but the life of the deep sea sailor is one of always keeping a step ahead of the hurricane season and we still had a long way to go.

Christmas Island and Cocos Keeling were heaven incarnate. Four months passed and we were still on the first page of our honeymoon and having a better time every day. Each day was a new adventure, everyday was a day to laugh and kiss on deserted beaches under the sun. On Christmas Island we hiked into the mountains and shared love beneath gigantic trees untouched since time began. On Direction Island in the Cocos group there was a cut in the reef that you dove into and then were swept past huge fish and sharks and beautiful corals by the current and then deposited right back next to your boat. Do things like this only happen on honeymoons?

Sooner or later it had to happen. We returned to civilization when we arrived in Galle, Sri Lanka. (Darwin could never be described as civilization, The Outback, the never never, the place all the way at the end of the goddamn road, where the 'old west' went to; but never civilization.

Civilization assumes that you have laws and that at least some of the citizens are sober, part of the day. Hey, Aussies, I'm joking!)

Galle in those days was the expatriate's dream. With a thousand a month you could live like a real king. Hot and cold running servants, carried on a throne chair to your own private beach to swim, 20 bedroom guest cottage, girls dropping grapes in your mouth, the whole nine yards. We didn't have any where near a thousand a month but we had a great time anyway. The snake in this Eden was the war that had been going on for 7000 years between the Tamils and the Buddhists. Mostly they didn't bother sailors. Mostly.

There is a dance, particular to yachtsmen, performed in every country in the world. This is the dance of clearing customs. Every country you sail to plays by the same rules.

The way of the dance is this. First you present yourself and your boat for inspection by appearing in their port and raising your yellow hankie. Yellow quarantine flag if you must. They pretend to be not interested in doing their job for which they are paid unless you promise a midnight kiss, a tip. Eventually they show up, do their duty and wait for their kiss.

Karen was a master of the dance. In Sri Lanka, two boat boys brought out the authorities and wanted a tip. They hinted at cigarettes. Karen was very reluctant to spread the use of drugs. When pressured by these two boat boys she offered one cigarette. They expected a pack if not a carton and since there were two of them, two of everything. She waved at them to give back her cigarette. They obeyed with alacrity. Instead of offering two packs, she tore her cigarette in half and offered both boys a half of a smoke. They were so flabbergasted they didn't know what to do so they rowed away in confusion.

We visited the Kandy, high up in the tea region. I wanted to buy Karen an engagement ring. Yes, it was a wee bit late but still for 86 dollars we bought a star sapphire mounted between two diamond chips; everyone who saw it was polite enough to be impressed. I love buying jewelry in the third world. Everyone bargains and enjoys it. I had our jeweler down to 91 dollars and he wouldn't budge further. I suggested we toss a coin. If he won, it would be 96 dollars. But if I won it would be 86 dollars. He agreed and I started to pull a coin from my pocket.

"No, Sahib. It has to be a neutral coin." We dragged a passer-by off the street and made him toss a coin from his pocket. Even though I won, every one had a great time. The jeweler made tea, the passer-by went and bought some sticky buns and I supplied the enhancement (gin, as we were still in the British Empire, kind of) for the tea. We all admired the beauty of Karen with her ring. What a great memory. Why do we in the west have to always be in such a big hurry? We miss so much in life. There can be so much joy in the little things.

We traveled, staying in guest cottages which were very, very basic but were only a dollar a night. Once Karen got sick with the flu and I went to the local pharmacy where they sold me a lotion to put on her third eye. The third eye, it seems, is the cause of the flu and can be located a fourth of the way between the top of the head and the eyes. If you feel around up there, they told me, you can find a soft spot. Or maybe they were just having fun with an American.

When for some strange, eerie, unknown reason the lotion didn't work, I walked around till I found the local speakeasy. It was hard to find, Sri Lanka being half Muslim. They had some real rotgut homebrew but it fixed Karen right up by burning the hell out of anything in there that got in its way.

On the way to climb 8,000 foot Sri Pada, or Adam's Peak in Western Civilization, we had to catch a school bus. On board were Tamil and Buddhist children. They sat together, played together; they were best friends. We asked them why their parents hated each other. Was it political? Was it religious? They had no explanation other than all parents are flawed.

Sri Pada was worth it. We climbed the mountain at night on Karen's birthday in order to greet the dawn. The dawn seen from such a perfect cone was supposed to convert the pagan and guarantee entrance into the afterlife for the devoted. Sri Pada is held holy in four different religions and each believe the footprint on its summit was caused by: Adam by the Christians, Buddha by the Buddhists, Mohammed by the Muslims and Vishnu by the Hindus. The good part was that in a war torn land the mountain was a haven of peace, respected by all sides. The sunrise was spectacular and the shadow of the mountain was beautifully reflected on the clouds and tea plantations below. I am still waiting to be canonized but Karen is set, she attained sainthood instantly when she married me!

We were so close we had to go to India. If Sri Lanka was old world charm in spades then India was old world charm doubled with exclamation points! On our way up the west coast, every little town had fishermen with different kinds of hats that varied wildly. Every hat she saw, Karen wanted. About this time Karen started to get moody. She would be cheerful one day and then crabby the next, so in a moment of pure insanity I threw her birth control pills overboard.

"Well, that is just fine, Mike, real fine. Now what are we going to do about making love or are you telling me that you want to start a baby?"

"It's alright, Karen. This is India. Every one in the world is trying to stop Indians from having more kids. There are going to be tons of birth control methods available. Not to worry."

But it wasn't true. Only Depo-Provera was available. This was a shot that was given once every 3 months and that worked well in preventing conception but was very hard on a woman's body. Finally in one clinic the nurse admitted that she did have some condoms. She went into the dark recesses of long tall shelves and eventually returned blowing dust off a big plastic bag.

"Here you go then, might as well take the whole bag. We don't want the little ones haunting our dreams, now do we?"

Thanking her gratefully we returned to the boat only to discover that our bag of condoms had been invaded by a colony of ants which were attracted to the talc. Karen threw out all the condoms that had ant holes in them.

Goa wasn't even really India. It had been a Portuguese colony for centuries and had just become part of India 20 years before. It was different in many ways.

Rum and other alcohols were openly for sale. Christianity was the prevailing religion, in fact Saint Francis Xavier's body, which had never decomposed, was still entombed in the cathedral where he is taken out on a throne and is the star in a parade once every 10 years.

We anchored off a five star hotel. This wasn't just any hotel. In the bathroom instead of paper towels there were piles of ironed linen towels! The lobby was lined with priceless Persian rugs and the gardens were unreal. I bought Karen lunch at the restaurant. They came out with the rice first and started to ladle it on to Karen's plate. She didn't know she was supposed to indicate when she had enough. The rice on her plate resembled a mountain as the server continued to pile it on! The help kept staring at her from around corners. They had never seen someone so hungry!

The hotel was kind enough to let us use their pool showers. To return the favor twice a week when they had beach dancing we showed up and got the ball rolling. The Indians, at least the ones that could afford a hotel like that, are very conservative. After cutting up together on the empty dance floor for a few numbers, I picked an older lady and Karen a man. For every new number we picked new partners. It didn't take that long to turn a boring dance into a jump up!

One night as a thank you the hotel held a dance contest. We danced our hearts out laughing the whole time. They gave us the prize- a bottle of wine which we drank as soon as we got back to the boat. We were really wasted! Normally we used our condoms when making love but we were too happy to remember, later on, if we did or didn't. Or else we did but Karen didn't find all of the ant holes! Anyway that, Dear Readers, was the night Falcon got started.

Tola Hauled out in Goa

THE PREGNANCY

The North East Monsoon had started. It was time to go, time to leave Goa and cross the Arabian and head up the Red Sea. This was the good monsoon, blowing out of Mongolia; it brought clear skies and fair winds from Asia; from the North East. The Arabian Sea was a beautiful sail for us. We were lucky. It was so clear and the swells were so low that Karen could play solitaire at night by the light of the full moon while on watch in the cockpit. She prided herself, that when she steered off course to avoid the occasional squall, she could ease back to the rhumb line by the next day's sextant noon sight. The approach to Aden was out of the Arabian Nights. The mountains around the port stacked one on top of the other till they looked like a huge palace from 10 miles at sea.

Aden was a very big Muslim port. It was fun to walk the streets full of bullet pocketed buildings. The grocery stores had almost nothing in them. In one store the size of a Safeway there was one pair of shoes. That was it, hundreds of shelves, one pair of shoes. Eventually we did manage to stock the boat up buying 'free food aid' that was illegally for sale under the counter. The canned Danish cheese was especially good. At the far end of town there were ancient huge brick pools built to hold millions of gallons of water. No one knew who built them or why, there in the desert where there is never any water or rain.

I think Karen knew she was pregnant. We looked around for a lady's doctor, but no, all the doctors were out on the front lines of the inevitable border disputes. She worried about getting fresh veggies, just
in case she was carrying. Eventually we found the Russian supermarket, well stocked for the Russian 'Advisors'. The funny part was they only accepted American dollars, even from their own countrymen!

We carried on up the Red Sea. What a ride! It blew like hell out in the open sea and then we anchored behind little islands where we swam with manta rays in water so crystal blue it rivaled the Bahamas. Sometimes we shared anchorages with smuggler/pirate boats. They were beautiful craft, their bows soaring above the deck designed to make way against the heavy conditions common in this part of the world. Their sterns were low in the water with big, big exhaust pipes. They had very serious engines. But they didn't bother us. First, what would a 24 foot boat have that they would want? Second, whenever one came close I broke out my anti-pirate gear. This consisted of my machete and a sharpening stone. I would just sit there in the cockpit, sharpen my machete and give them evil looks.

It was an elegant solution. If I had a gun I could be a threat to them and they would then take action. If I tried to run away I would be prey and I would be chased. If I screamed and yelled I would be a nuisance and would be squished. Everyone respects the little dog that stands his ground and defends his turf. The Muslim mind respects courage.

Karen's anti-pirate plan was to invite the pirates on board and offer them tea and cookies relying on the Muslim law forbidding a guest from harming his host! Luckily we never met any marauding pirates; or at least we didn't until the Suez Canal.

A couple more weeks of lovely cruising from little island to little island stopped when we arrived in Port Sudan, the half way point on our journey up the Big Red and where the wind would now be against us. In the port there was always a guard at the dinghy dock to make sure no one brought liquor ashore to give or sell to the Muslim locals. The guard made a big thing out of pawing through any woman's bags. He ignored the men. One experience was enough for Karen. The next time she went ashore, when the guard motioned her over to his table she put her bag on the ground and motioned to him to come over and go through it at her feet. They motioned back and forth for ten minutes. Karen was determined to have respect. Sometimes not   having a common language can be a blessing! Finally the guard gave up and waved her to go on her way and didn't bother her again.

One of the great things to do in those days in Port Sudan, besides going out for donut holes at dawn to the center of town where men sat around frying the dough on open fires and discussing the world, was going to the thieves' markets. They really weren't thieves. They were religious refugees from mostly Moslem Eritrea which was then at war with mostly Christian Ethiopia. What little money they had was spent getting out of their war torn country to then relatively safe Sudan. Often they left only hours before they would be killed so they were selling what heirlooms they managed to pack to survive.

I set my heart on a Berber Sword. Berbers are white North Africans who roam the desert and are so fierce that even the Arabs fear them. Their swords are a meter long and appear wider at the tip than at the shaft. These are the swords that defeated the Crusaders by being so sharp they would cut through even heavy armor.

Karen and I visited the market one Tuesday on a busy day ashore. We were fighting fate by trying to accomplish more than one thing on any given day. We had already been to the market and were on the way to the lady-baby doctor when we passed the thieves' square. Soon we found what we were looking for and were deciding which of ten available swords to buy when a crowd developed. It seemed that to pick a good blade one had to hear it sing. These guys had such well developed forearms that they could just squeeze their hands on the handle and set up a resonant vibration along the blade producing a beautiful tone. Twenty men were around us and all had to have a try. We were all making grunting noises and nodding our heads, acting like men anywhere in the world, don't you know.

Karen was feeling left out so she decided to have a try and reached out her hand for a sword. As one, twenty hands half pulled their own personal swords out of their scabbards and a once babbling market crowd became suddenly deathly silent. Quickly Karen pulled her hand back and whispered to me, "I think I'll give it a go back on the boat!" I ended up buying a sword and we carried on to the doctor. It is not an urban myth but a sea going one that sailors can only accomplish one major thing a day, completely successfully. The rule is, get something done and then before disaster strikes, find a bar, quick! If not, the myth goes, anything attempted after that is doomed to at least partial failure; except on that rare lucky day when everything just seems to go right. This was one of those days.

On reaching the Doctor's, Karen was placed on a bed and a curtain drawn in front of her at the end of a long single room dwelling. The doctor examined her from the man's side, feeling her tummy through the cloth. After five minutes the British educated Doctor walked, no, almost crawled over to me from the far side of the room, his eyes on the floor, bowing, and his hands pressed tightly together as sweat gathered on his brow.

"Please, Sir. May I draw the curtain? I just want to be sure everything is all right with your lady. Please, Sir, please." Casually I nodded my consent and went back to swishing my sword back and forth while trying to get it to sing and attempting to grunt with an Arab accent all at the same time!

The doctor confirmed that Karen was pregnant and the mountain of parenthood loomed ahead of us. Karen was totally overjoyed. She already knew that she was pregnant and went to the doctor just to please me. She swore she even knew which time did it. Well, I kind of had my suspicions too!

Most of our friends sailing their boats up the Red Sea in the same season as we, would hide during the strong gales and as soon as it fell calm would motor like hell and hide again as soon as the wind started to build. We, being engineless, didn't have that option. We sat anchored during the calms and sailed during the gales. Little Karen took it like a trooper. At times, the seas were so rough that the keel came out of the water, all the way back to the rudder, before the boat came smashing down again. These were the Red Sea's famous square waves that were famed to have made more people give up sailing than seas anywhere else in the world. At times we would be becalmed in the middle of the sea and in the shipping lanes. There were a lot of ships, sometimes as many as 20 in sight at a given time, a very dangerous situation. So we would drop the dinghy in the water and I would tow Tola along while Karen alternated between steering and sculling with a long sweep. I attached a 10 foot section of 3/8" chain to a line off the dinghy and the other end to Tola's bow. That way the dinghy wasn't towing the boat, the chain was, as the dinghy pulled the other end of the chain. It eliminated the jerking of the tow line one usually got from a dinghy. The annoying part was that it didn't matter how far we got out of the shipping lanes, the ships would see us rowing along and change course to come and look at us!

Sometimes it was a nice day, for the Big Red that is, and then it would blow up from 20 to 25 to 35 gusting to 50 knots in just a few minutes. One such time we made the mistake of heading for the nearest shelter. It was a narrow Marsha (a fiord- like inlet, fiord-like below the water anyway, narrow, steep and deep. Above the water it was flat desert with occasional low hills.) The Marsha didn't have any soundings marked on our chart. That didn't mean that it had no useable bottom. Our charts were photocopies of photocopies and sometimes details got lost in translation, this Marsha was charted on the crease where the chart had been folded and few details could be discerned. This was a situation we normally would have avoided, but it was nasty out and a possible anchorage was right there, 3 miles under our lee. I know old salts are always saying that the most dangerous thing to do at sea is to approach land in nasty weather, I knew it. Absolutely, I knew it, but I decided to go take a look anyway. Sometimes I think I have a death wish or something, I do such stupid things.

The inlet was fairly narrow but not more so than most and the waves settled down a bit as we closed the coast but the wind also clocked more northerly following the land till it was blowing straight out of the inlet. We were down to a triple reefed main, a storm jib and were heavily pressed. We tacked back and forth across the entrance sometimes not coming about till we were 10 or 20 feet from the breaking reefs on either side but still we were making little progress. The water that was breaking over the reefs was rushing out the entrance and trying to flush us out of the marsha. We finally got in far enough to find the bottom at 50 feet and we were so tired that I decided to anchor right in the middle of the inlet. I dropped my best

CQR and ran out the rode to the knot. It didn't help. We were slowly dragging merrily along and right towards the reef. We quickly launched the dinghy and I rowed out a big hi-tensile danforth with 300 feet of line and 50 feet of chain and hand set it. That held. But who knew for how long? With only 50 feet of chain the line could easily be rubbing against some coral down there. So from the dinghy I started pulling up the CQR. I didn't want to raise it from the boat as I might upset the delicate balance of the danforth. At one time I had both the CQR and the chain aboard the dinghy until I was swamped and sunk by

a breaking wave. I quickly jettisoned the anchor to lighten ship, bailed the dinghy out and tried again. Now the chain had fouled itself around a coral head and I had to dive down to get the chain back foot by foot. Eventually we got everything back on Tola and started to worry about the danforth. The wind had been increasing all through the day and was now gusting over 50 knots. The reefs were a boat length behind the stern. If the anchor gave way or the line broke we would lose Tola for sure. So we pulled up the sails and the anchor, which came up way too easily, and sailed back, down wind, to the port we had left that morning, totally exhausted mentally and physically. Such was our life in the Big Red.

On those really windy days we normally would hide in port and listen as the wind in the rigging set up a different harmonic moan for each stay and shroud. It was strangely soothing and yet haunting at the same time. That combined with the tear drop sunsets are my most visceral memories of the Red Sea. Some of the Marshas were memorable too. Once anchored, we would go for a hike to see what we could see. Often we were invited for a meal by the inevitable guards on camelback that were there to keep us from attacking the desert. Sometimes we would find ruins with old glass bottles and strange lab equipment and we would ask ourselves why on earth anyone would build something like that in such an inhospitable place.

At the top of the Red Sea is the Gulf of Suez, the toughest part of all to sail. The winds are stronger and there is less room to tack back and forth. What I didn't know was that the Gulf was filled with oil well platforms. I remember one night that was magic. It was blowing about 25 knots, headwinds of course; the whole sky was filled with blood red light from the burn off on top of the oil rigs. There were ships everywhere, there were platforms every ½ mile, there were unlit pipes sticking out here and there, and we had to sail through it! Karen wanted to know if she could help, but I told her to just keep the coffee coming, I was having a ball tacking this way and that! Sometimes that night, I didn't know if I had gone to hell from reading too much Dante or if I was in sailing heaven.

The next morning we arrived in Port Suez and I hit the hay. Soon the pirates, sorry, ship agents, started to arrive. They were ramming each other and Tola trying to get close enough to get our business for the transit of the Suez Canal. I woke up from all the racket and stuck my head up out of the hatch. There was Karen swinging our Sudanese sword this way and that, swearing at them, that if they scratched her paint, she would stick 'em. And, damn, she had gotten that sword to sing!

We picked the 'Prince of the Red Sea' as our agent, and we could not have been introduced to the Muslim world of Egypt by a nicer man. I think it helped that Karen was pregnant. He showered her with gifts, took us out for lunch many times, and arranged for our transit of engineless Tola (technically illegal), and gave me a refund on our transit. We were towed through by a sand barge. What a blast! The barge had a 6 foot long rudder behind it's prop that almost broke the surface. It was just wide enough that Karen could veer us over to it and I would jump from Tola's bow and walk on top of the rudder to go and visit the barge. To the ships that were passing, it looked like I was walking on water. On the barge, we had a blast drinking tea and grunting. Grunting is the universal man language in the world. No matter where one goes a grunt made in a certain way means the same. Mostly we grunted about how beautiful our boats were and how terrible all the big ships passing us looked.

Larnaca in Cyprus was back to the yachtie way of life. Find the cheapest good restaurant in town where everyone goes together to tell stories of the Red Sea and the Med all night long. Of course they all expected us to give up sailing and go back to America to have the baby. Karen surprised them all by stating,

"They have babies everywhere. Sometimes the babies are born in fields as the mother is working. It is not an illness. It is as natural as eating and breathing."

But where we were going to have the baby was another question. It was the end of April and the baby was due in August when it was very hot in the Med. Many mothers suggested we stay in Cyprus where the living was easy and it wasn't overly expensive. Karen, however, wanted to sail the Med and see some sights before the kid joined our honeymoon.

In Larnaca we met 'Aquilla', a 50 foot home built catamaran with 4 kids on board. They were all home schooled and doing great. Lucy in particular was a whiz at math. One of the struggles of cruising and particularly in the Med, in those days, was the constantly changing currencies. To know if something was a good buy, the cost of the item must be converted into your home currency and then reconverted into the last country's currency to decide if it was a good buy or not. Lucy could do this in her head in seconds, at 10 years of age, with no formal education. Karen, a professional teacher, you will remember, just watched and remembered and smiled.

Our next stop was Turkey. What a great country for motoring! We sat on the south coast for 5 days. The wind came up and we made progress, and then it died and the current took us back. The coast was solid cliffs and very deep, so we couldn't anchor. Karen had to put up with my mumbling under my breath about how I was going to put a huge motor on this boat. Finally, we were rescued by another sailboat whom we had met in Cyprus. We had almost made it into Fethiye, but were glad of the tow. Who really knew how much longer we would have been out there? In Marmaris, Karen had an ultra sound to make sure everything was copasetic. The kid seemed normal but was shy and hid his or her sex. For some reason she wouldn't let me come into the office this time with her. I didn't even have my sword with me.

As all parents do, we had been trying to come up with a name but couldn't reach an agreement. Karen was holding out for Sean if it was a boy and I for Jack. As a joke we started referring to the baby as Abdul. If it was a girl Karen wanted Shannon Rose and I, Joann. As a nickname she would be Scheherazade or Zady for short!

While we were there we met a nice couple who wanted to sail to Cyprus but were a little nervous about the whole thing but would pay us to help and give them a few pointers. The only problem is they wanted to leave right now and had already checked out of the country. I thought for a few minutes and then said we do it, figuring we would solve the custom and immigration quagmire later. It was a great sail the only black point was that they expected pregnant Karen to cook and stand a watch. She soon set them right, one or the other watch but not both. I was starting to learn, as our first wedding anniversary approached, that the main survival technique for our marriage was never mess with The Karen. They sent us back by ferry to Rhodos which was like being on a cruise ship and gave us some money to take the little ferry back to our boat in Marmaris, where we hadn't checked out of properly.

At the time we hadn't seen 'Midnight Express' and really didn't realize the danger we were in, but St. Jude, the patron saint for the hopelessly insane and sailors, some how got us through. As all the ferry passengers stood in line to clear customs we migrated to the back of the line hoping for a miracle but none appeared. We finally bellied up to the window which got us an armed guard and a trip to the commandant's office. There, an older, impeccably dressed officer asked us what we thought we were doing breaking the laws of Turkey. I explained the best I could which resulted with him hitting the desk with his Billy-club a few times, an act that after we saw the movie was meant to terrify us. We sat in his office sweating but eventually he let us go with a fine.

In Greece, where we went next, the child to be was nick-named Alexander as we still couldn't agree on a name. We were starting to feel like Mary and Joseph trying to find an inn for the birth so we decided that Greece was as good a place as any. That was before we discovered that if it was to be a boy and even as an American, he still could be drafted into the Greek military as he would be Greek born. Also 75% of Greek women have cesarean deliveries. That set Karen off and she ranted and raved about women rights and lazy doctors for a couple of days.

So we decided to go to Malta. Our good friend on Caymanifique had had back surgery at the hospital there and was full of praise. They spoke English in Malta, which they didn't in Greece and the marina was reported to be better. The problem was that Karen was 8 months pregnant. It was her first child. Apparently it could pop out at any time. When we announced our decision to head for Malta, sage heads around the marina wagged, signal flags were raised and smoke blew out of scores of captain's ears.

Stories of our 5 days of going nowhere off of Turkey without an engine were repeated endlessly.

Dr. Jim took the assignment of heading the persuasion invasion force and to be fair he did it with class. To get us to stay in Greece he took me aside one afternoon and explained every possible disaster scenario that could happen in childbirth, in graphic detail. To his credit he also explained what to do about it, with lots of, 'in this case you must seek the nearest hospital immediately.' He explained that since it was her first birth it was quite likely that the baby would arrive as much as 4 weeks early.

Karen and I talked it over. She recognized the dangers but worried more about the horrors of the Greek midwives. We had visited a Greek hospital to check out the situation and watched in horror as the midwife took a newborn baby and washed him under a freezing cold facet. I put my hand under it. It was really cold! It seems that Alexander the Great was washed as a newborn in a cold mountain stream and so sentenced the entire Greek nation to follow in his footsteps. We had been to Turkey, Cyprus and Greece and still had not found a place for the birth. We started to think about the advantages and disadvantages of the baby's future nationality. He would be an American with a passport listing him as 'an American born over seas,' but he could also take on the nationality of the country he was born in. We thought about what his or her life would be like and wondered if we could give the baby a leg up in life by picking wisely a birth country. Karen was a bi-national, an American and a New Zealander, so the baby would inherit Karen's New Zealand nationality at least till 18, when some authorities say he must choose. But that was many years down the road. The interesting thought was what the world would look like 18 years from now.

When we found out that if a boy was born in Greece and years later if he passed through Greece, even if he was a totally different nationality and on an international flight and remaining on the plane for the next leg, he could be pulled off the plane and inducted into the Greek Army! We still didn't know the fetus's sex but Karen was hoping for a boy so that freaked her out. Malta it was going to be.

It started out as a good voyage. We had a fair wind and made an amazing, for the Med and a 24-foot boat, up wind and up current, 78 miles the first day noon to noon. The next day wasn't as good or the next. I was seriously getting worried.

"Karen, we are going to have to head north to Athens. At this rate we will not make it to Malta in time. You are already eight and a half months gone and there are just too many things that can go wrong."

"Silly, silly Mike. Don't you know that it takes 280 days or almost 10 months to grow a baby? I'm only 240 days gone."

"I thought it was 9 months, in fact I am sure it is."

"And who are you going to believe, some silly text book written by a man or a woman bearing a child?"

We made the voyage in 10 days and Karen gave birth 30 days later right at 280 days. Who knew? Why don't they tell us men these things?

It wasn't an easy birth. I sweated the whole time thinking of what might have happened if Karen had given birth at sea. It started out well enough. I had organized a car but, of course, it didn't show up when I called. I flagged down a taxi and it turned out that the driver's wife had given birth just the week before at the same hospital. He told us not to worry. He would take us to the back entrance. We laughed and enjoyed the moment. Ignorance is such bliss. I'm glad we had that moment before reality loomed over us.

"Much shorter. Save much walking for the Madam. Trust me," our volunteer driver told us. We went down dark alleys and up strange streets. I started to wonder if we were being taken for a ride but when we arrived the driver would take no money.

"You are going to need your money. Trust me."

Karen only had to wait 2 hours to become dilated and 7 hours after that we had a baby boy. Then the trouble started. Karen had pushed so hard that she had ruptured herself and was bleeding uncontrollably, internally. The little nurse didn't know what to do. I called on my best captain voice and told her to get a doctor right now. Of course she disappeared and no one came. I went totally ballistic.

> An old rule of the navy is:
> When in danger or doubt
> Run in circles, scream, and shout.

By the time I had finished shouting and screaming up and down every wing of the hospital twice, I had the head of surgery, the whole ER team and five or six extra doctors for luck. They had her under the knife for four hours before everything was fixed, the poor little thing.

Just after our son was born this very officious nurse got right up in my face and asked what was the baby's name. Karen and I still hadn't decided, partially because the baby had always hidden its sex during ultrasounds. We had nicknamed the fetus 'Falcon' this time as we didn't know anything else that went with Malta. It couldn't be Abdul and Scheherazade no longer applied. I told the nurse that we hadn't decided yet. Undeterred the nurse demanded harshly, "What is the baby's name?" I looked at Karen and asked "Falcon"? At that time she was so happy that it was over (she thought) that I could have said Beelzebub and she would have agreed. So he officially became Falcon Alexander Riley. The next day I registered Falcon's birth with the locals and the official made a big thing out of Falcon's initials.

"F.A.R. He will see far in his life," I was told with a wise nod from his ancient head.

Karen spent 5 days in the hospital, the 'Hotel' she called it. I liked going to visit. Each baby was in his own little bubble of a cart and we fathers were allowed to wheel our new charges up and down the hall. On the last day I walked into Karen's room with a crestfallen look on my face.

"What's wrong, Mike?" asked Karen with alarm growing on her face.

"I had to sell the boat to pay for the birth and the operation, Babe. I'm really sorry." The poor little thing started to cry so I couldn't keep up my deception any longer. "Honey, don't worry. I didn't sell the boat. The total bill was 50 American for everything. And they apologized that it was so much. His American passport cost more than his birth and your operation!"

Tears of sadness were replaced by tears of joy interspersed with glares. Aw, the things us men live for!

Jonathon, a buddy, fellow cruiser, and Falcon's godfather had a rental unit overlooking the sea that he lent to us for a week. I moved Karen into there which worked out well as the poor thing could hardly walk, she had so many stitches. We made a bed for Falcon out of a dresser drawer and lots of towels. He seemed very happy in his new berth so we stepped out on the balcony to enjoy the view only to be interrupted by blood-curdling screams. Falcon 5 days old had managed to roll over and was not very happy at all face down. We had a lot to learn about this parenting stuff.

Karen teaching school in Papua New Guinea

THE EARLY YEARS

When Falcon was twenty days old, we left Malta and headed for Tunisia. Most of the cruisers in Malta insisted that we should stay put in the marina in Malta, for the first year at least. Not one, or two, but people everywhere told us that we had to put the child first. They told us that our lives were going to be different now. We had to put away the toys and joys of early adulthood, and settle down to the toil and trouble of parenthood. This didn't make sense to me. I had spent a lot of years learning the way of the sea, learning the art of boatkeeping, finding the right girl to share my life with, and now, they tell me to give it all up? Sure, I knew it wasn't all about me anymore, if it ever was, but what could I offer my offspring if not myself? Was my son going to inherit my name but not the quirky personality that was his father? No, it seemed to me that my kid was the harmony to add to the melody of our lives. To me a child was not a burden, or someone to whom we should sacrifice our way of life. A son was someone to teach and guide in your own sense of living. I imagine all fathers must feel this, but somewhere along the way, they become distracted or sidetracked.

Well, people had attempted to change the course of my life since I was sailing my first dinghy in fourth grade. Perhaps they thought that they were making me into a man. Maybe, they wished to change me, or to reform that what was in me. Why? What is so wrong letting me

53

turn out just the way it happens? Sure, I respected that I had to be taught the basics of life. But, come on, everything you really need to know in life, you learn in kindergarten. Don't hit, don't take, stay together crossing the street, take a nap in the afternoon, say please and thank you. It doesn't have to be forced down your throat. Now, how was I going to bring up my kid? Was I going to be doomed to repeat the errors of my parents and teachers?

Our parents in absentia, the older group of cruising people in the marina in Malta, thought it was just too risky to take such a young child sailing. When we informed them that we were carrying on through the Med and across the Atlantic, they thought us very foolhardy risking the baby's health and life, and told us so repeatedly.

It wasn't that we took a lot of foolhardy risks. We didn't, as long as one didn't count sailing around the world on a 24-foot sailboat without an engine, risky. The point is that within the parameters of our lives we didn't take unnecessary risks. We waited till the light was green before crossing. We lived as safely as our lives would let us. We waited for a good forecast before making a big passage. We didn't go out of our way to antagonize the locals. Or, I should say, me. Karen didn't have to worry about antagonizing the locals. Everyone who met Karen instantly fell in love with her. She is one of those people whom make instant friends whist standing in the grocery line, and if the line has more than 3 people ahead of her, she will hear at least one person's life history before she gets to the checkout counter. It isn't something that she encourages. People just naturally gravitate towards her. As for me on the other hand...

I grew up aggressive. As I matured I became more independent. I received so much bad advice as a young man that I quickly decided that if I was going to make mistakes, they would be mine. And I did make mistakes, a lot of them. I loved taking risks back then. I always crossed the street on the red. The words 'no' or 'can't' or 'never' were red flags to me. By the time I was 37, I was or had been an industrial spy, a car ferry captain, an ex-convict, a penguin breeder, a businessman, a long liner and gill net fisherman, a whale hunter, a dolphin and sea lion collector, a microbiologist, and had developed a steely look to my eyes that put fear into men and melted women in their tracks. There is no doubt that by 50, I would have been dead.

Meeting Karen, and becoming a father, changed me. My aggression became protective. I didn't care what people said, only what Karen said. Somehow, Karen talked me out of mistakes before they happened. My steely look was lost; no, Karen says it is still there, just better hidden by a very thin veneer of civilization.

When I was very young, long, long before I even dreamed of meeting Karen, I went to jail. But not on purpose! I had been an avid reader of the James Bond novels and loved the TV series, 'It Takes a Thief,' so when the chance came to do a bit of spying, I jumped at the chance! It was so romantic! I was living a dream. And all I had to do was take photos! Unfortunately, the police didn't consider it romantic. Neither did they think it was spying. It was breaking and entering and burglary and threatened to send me to prison for 5 long years. It ironed out the last of my illusions about life. Luckily, I managed to talk myself into a halfway house after 6 months and started a new part of my life, dedicated to freedom. Freedom from all authority. Let me tell you, if you resent obeying, at times, nonsensical traffic laws, try going to prison. It will change your perspective. Suddenly, all authority was but a reminder of the worse six months of my life.

Did prison change me? Oh, yeah. Did it change me to the better? Define better. What I dedicated my life to on my release from prison was to separating myself from authority as much as possible, to live my life as I wished to live it, to bow before no man as much as possible. So I returned to the sea and have remained there ever since.

Anyway, back to Malta, the thing is, that when everyone said, stay, be careful, don't take risks, that steely look rose from the primal depths and I just looked at them like the bunch of wimps that they were.

Of course, it didn't help that the day after Falcon's birth an Italian motor yacht zoomed into the marina at 20 knots throwing a wall of water that had all the boats med moored against the sea wall, crashing up against the rocks. I had been in major party mode all day and wasn't about to put up with any foolishness. To be fair, no one else was either. I returned from the hospital with news of joy and relief and I started drinking. Starting with Caymanifique moored next door, I had a drink on every boat in the harbor. Then the Italian tidal wave arrived, 40 of us cruisers ran up to where the tsunami maker was tying up. Boy, were we mad! I just kept thinking that if my little baby had been on board he might have been thrown onto the floor by the commotion. One young man jumped from the Italian boat and was tying up the stern lines. I threw him in the water and tossed off his lines. We were all shouting and yelling, 'Italians go home,' you know, that kind of thing. A big fight started, which finally ended when the Port Captain threw the wake maker out of Malta, and blacklisted him.

The more moderate of the cruising folk didn't approve of me or my actions at all, and made no bones about telling me so. They told me I was irresponsible and not worthy of parenthood. Wouldn't it be great if we were all laughing fellow rovers, sailing the seven seas? Those among us who looked on life as a grand and great adventure were few indeed.

I thought our first stop should be Tunisia. Libya and Tunisia had just opened their common border, and the Libyans were allowed to cross over to work and to buy the many things that their then oppressive regime had prevented them from doing and getting. Going there did sound risky, but the lure was that prices were very reasonable and a haul out for the boat was $100 American up and down and a free week of lay days. That, in case you are wondering, or don't know, is a really, really good price. We fathers had to be conservative with our pennies. Besides it was on the way, well, kind of, and we could stop and see Carthage, or at least what the Romans had left of it after the Punic Wars.

The moderates in the marina in Malta were outraged that we would take a two week old baby to a country 'overrun' by terrorists from Libya. Come on! Get a life! These were just regular people coming from Libya, looking for a TV or whatever to buy. They were not their government. They weren't even Italians! Besides did they expect us to huddle in the hut by the fire, shivering and waiting, till the wolves and barbarians tore down our door? The first thing you learn in the big house is that fear is an invitation to attack. Predators can smell it and like sharks, will attack mindlessly. The one way to be sure to be attacked is to show fear, whether you are a man, a family, or a country.

Back on track, Tunisia was fun. We hauled out down by the border. Not only was it cheaper but it also had a Turkish bath for the yard's showers! Think of it. After a hard day sanding, scraping and painting, we showered, then lay around in a heated pool and steam room for an hour. That is the way to run a boat yard!

We made a portable crib out of a piece of plywood that Karen sewed up sides and made handles for with sunbrella. We saw no signs of terrorists. The only hint that they might be there was that the police stopped us at least once every couple of days thinking that we were carrying a bomb in the strange sunbrella luggage we had! When they found out it was a baby, their fierce demeanor changed to that of loving and happy protectors. Often they would go into the nearest store and buy him a little trinket.

In Sidi Bou Said, I found work repairing a sailor's boat whose mast had collapsed his deck from over tensioning of the shrouds. Because it was illegal to work in Tunisia, I had to supervise only. I hired the men and organized the job. Sometimes, I wanted so much to pick up a tool and show the workmen how to do the job, but there were eyes everywhere. I spent most of my time running over to Tola, docked 150 feet away, to ask Karen how to say different things in French, which was the local lingua, and then ran back with fresh instructions for my crew before I forgot how to say them.

The owner of the boat was a bigwig from Germany and we spent a lot of time drinking wickedly strong coffee in little cups at the local restaurant. He was convinced that his wife was a Russian spy. She used to be a ballerina in Moscow but gave it all up when she met him, while he was working there. He first started to wonder when he found her calling her 'girl friends' in the middle of the night while he was sleeping. But what a looker and what a body! She fell in love with Karen (naturally) and Falcon, and gave them baby clothes that her own 2 year old had outgrown.

The only trouble we had with Falcon was when we bought a kilo of beautiful huge grapes. Karen must have needed the vitamins and minerals in them as she ate the whole kilo by herself on the bus returning from the market before she could stop herself. The next day, was Falcon ever fussy with the colic. I don't think he appreciated the change in his milk!

Carthage was fun but dusty, Tunis was dusty and busy; everywhere the people were great, but we were eager to get back on the boat again and back to Europe. The great thing about ocean traveling is the quiet time at sea, lets you recover from the hustle and bustle of land. Even when the sea is rough it is still a nice change from land.

And when it's stormy, it makes us appreciate land all the more.

Quickly we went through the Balearics and mainland Spain. It was starting to get cold. We had to wear sweaters during the day. In Motril we had heard of a garden or palace called Alhambra. We took the bus 50 miles inland, which delighted Karen, as she loved to get off the boat and see the country. It was a real carnival getting Falcon, his stuff and ourselves on and off the bus, one that we would become quite expert at over the years. In honor of the occasion we bought a 12 wheel umbrella baby carriage. The salesgirl almost refused to sell it to us. She insisted that Falcon was too young to be sitting up and we should have a proper ($500) carriage. Karen tried to explain about our lack of space but to no avail. I finally insisted that we would always drive on the back axle while he was in it and we beat a strategic retreat. Back in Alhambra we found out it was $10 a piece to get into the gardens so we returned to the boat after a nice bus ride. Years later when we found out how very special Alhambra really is, I did some serious butt kicking. Mine.

The southern coast of Spain is famed for its smugglers. No, they don't smuggle drugs or guns. Wait. Let me take that back. They do smuggle drugs; cigarettes. One dark night 10 miles offshore in 6 knots of following wind, we heard really big engines but we couldn't see any running lights anywhere. They were very noisy and were getting louder and louder. We quickly turned on every light we had all over the boat but still the engines became louder. We were sure we were about to be run over by cigarette smugglers when a huge spotlight illuminated us from out of nowhere. Finally, seeing no threat, they turned on their ship's lights and we were boarded by the Spanish Coastal Patrol. They were fairly gruff until Karen brought out from the cabin a waking up and crabby Falcon. After a cursory search they sent us on our way. I guess smugglers don't ship with infants!

In Gibraltar the grocery store was on the other side of the airfield from the harbor. We had a traffic light to tell us when it was safe to cross the field. Sometimes when the tower saw Falcon in his baby carriage they would make us wait extra long till it was absolutely safe. I really didn't mind and I know Falcon didn't. Some of the world's most exotic planes passed within a few feet of our eyes, and they weren't even charging us for it! Falcon didn't seem to mind the noise of the engines. Would he one day be a pilot? Would he go to the Air force Academy; would he be a Falcon playing for the Falcons?

My parents visited us on Tenerife in the Canaries. I had sent them pictures of both Karen and Falcon but I think they still wanted to see for themselves this girl I met in New Guinea to be sure I didn't fake the photos. I think they thought she was from the Highlands with a bone through her nose! They knew we were going to be in the Canaries around the first of December but didn't know which of the islands we were going to visit. This didn't stop them. They flew into Las Palmas on Grand Canary while, little known to them, we were on Tenerife. Not finding us in the harbor they found a boat with a ham radio on board and sent out a health and welfare inquiry. The next day they were sitting in Tola's cockpit very relieved at Karen's western beauty. Now those two are real adventurers.

Crossing the Atlantic in a 24 footer is always fun but rolly. Falcon surprised us with his knack for wedging himself in a corner and hanging on with one hand while playing with a toy with the other. When Karen first came on board I gave her a little locker for her belongings, one out of maybe 70 lockers on board. I told her that as she became more accomplished in sailing she would get more lockers. By the time Falcon came on board she 'owned' four personal lockers to my three and wanted more for Falcon.

Do you know how much space infants need? And we aren't even talking about diapers! One good thing that came out of the locker school is that Karen became really, really good at packing an amazing amount of gear into a very small space.

I really didn't have much to do with Falcon's education during these years. It was really his mother's time in the sun. I was just there as a support group to tell her what a great job she was doing and to bounce my son on my knee. It wasn't that I felt left out, more of the boat work was left to me which kept me busy repairing the ravages of the Atlantic. It came to me one day halfway across the ocean that if I had an official title I would be more important. Thus started the soon to be famed FSG. At the moment we were the only members of the Falcon Support Group. The mission of the group was not to do things for Falcon, but to support him in his efforts to do them himself. In time we enlisted hundreds in the group's noble cause.

After sailing thru the Caribbean and the Bahamas, we stopped on the west coast of Florida to visit Karen's parents in Venice and to hide from the upcoming hurricane season. Along the way we had to cross the Gulf Stream. We were becalmed 10 miles from Florida, naturally. It was interesting but frustrating to watch the coast pass in front of our eyes with the boat dead in the water. Eventually the wind returned after we had been carried a hundred miles north in the wrong direction!

On the way to Venice, we stopped at Pine Island to haul and paint the boat. We worried about the toxic chemicals around the yard and decided to put Falcon into day care. What a drama! Here is this little 18 month old kid, who has never been away from his parents for a second of his life, abandoned in a stranger's house! The tears and the crying! A hundred feet away from the house Karen broke down in tears also. Luckily, as president of the FSG, I had to stay dry eyed, mostly. The second day was a little better and by the end of the haul out, he couldn't wait for us to leave after dropping him off. So fickle, dependency!

Karen Weathering the Squalls

Educational Experience

Temper Tantrum

When Falcon was in Venice Florida, he joined the ranks of the terrible two's. Suddenly he had definite likes and dislikes and if he was shopping with us he was not shy in making his choices known, especially concerning frosted flakes. Any kind of sugar-coated flake would do as long as he could stuff it in his mouth instead of an apple.

One day, he decided he was tired of being Mr. Nice and Well-Brought-Up Kid, who liked what he got, and instead became The Kid From Hell, who got what he liked. In the grocery store (where else could he so embarrass his parents?), he let go with World War III or IV, what ever we are up to now, and performed a full-throttle, no-holds-barred, temper tantrum.

We were aghast at the change in behavior in the former beneficiary of our will. Everyone was staring at us. Quickly, I pulled him out of his stroller, which made him scream even louder, and took him outside. There we sat on a bench until he cried himself out. In between sobs he got it out, that he wanted to go back inside to his mother, who wanted to give him lots of cereal.

"As soon as you stop crying and decide to be a good boy then we can go back inside," I managed to relay to him. Eventually all things cease, even temper tantrums. We went back to the store and his stroller, I gave him an apple and a banana to hold, one for each hand and all was well in our world, momentarily.

A week later I had to pick up a dozen eggs from the same store. I had taken Falcon off the boat as he was fussy and giving his mother fits. He loved to ride in the car and usually fell asleep within 10 minutes in his car seat. By the time I got to the store he was fast asleep. Should I wake him up and risk another temper tantrum from a fussy child? He was sleeping so soundly, finally; however it was against Florida State law to leave an infant alone in a car. But if he didn't get some sleep he would be fitful all night, his mother would be cranky and your dear narrator wouldn't get any!

In the end I left him asleep in the car. I did lock the car and crack the windows. I rushed into the store, grabbed the eggs, and was standing in the checkout line when a voice came out over the loudspeaker,

"Will the owner of a red Honda Civic with the child in the back please return to your car?" I left the eggs on the counter and rushed out. There were 20 women crowded around the car terrorizing my kid. All had scowls on their faces; one was tapping on the window with a coin. Falcon was screaming a blue fit having woken from a nice sleep to a nightmare, where you are tied down to a chair, and are tormented by demons. Luckily, the women abandoned the car, surrounded me, and started screaming at me, telling me what an irresponsible father I was for leaving my kid in a car.

I should have jumped in the car and left but I was angry and ready for battle so I asked the women, which one of them was going to pay for my kid's psychoanalysis from the trauma caused by the witches who terrorized him this day. But they were making so much noise, and Falcon's continuing screams insured that the message didn't get through. But if any of you are reading this now, HA, I got in the last word.

_/) _/) _/)

Falcon had an easy time learning to walk. He started holding on to the sides of the settees in the salon down below. The settees were just at the right height for him to grasp. Because of the movement of the boat he didn't let go. The salon floor was 8 feet by 2½. With a lurch, he could let go of one side and lean over and grab the opposite side. We flew over to visit my parents and there he crawled for the first time. He had to. His mother was moving too fast and there was nothing to hold on to. He had to keep up. Falcon never had to crawl before as Tola was too small. Everything could be reached just by reaching out a hand. At my parents he crawled for 12 hours till he got a sore on his knee. After a bit of feeling sorry for himself and a present of a new pair of shoes from my mother, he was off and walking. Within a week, he was going downstairs without holding on. Hey, for him it was easy. This house didn't even move!

We had a nice hurricane season with no close approaches by storms and to our surprise were quite comfortable anchored out. We thought that the heat and humidity of Florida in the summer might become too much for us but we were acclimated. We bought a car which was fun even though the air conditioner didn't work.

Soon we were cruising again. We went around the west end of Cuba to the Cayman Islands where one of Falcon's god-parents lived. Stewart was the guy who told us way back in Greece about the hospital in Malta and we had been friends ever since. Back in Malta when Falcon was born we enlisted half the cruising fleet as god-parents just to have an excuse for a party. (Stewart and Isabel on board Caymanifique were two who kept in touch over the years.) It is funny how good friends stay good friends forever. In talking with Stewart and Isabel it was like we lived next door. There were no awkward silences. What great guys.

We started our run down to the canal with our fingers crossed. Like the Suez, the Panama Canal did not allow engineless sailboats to transit. Absolutely without exception. What would we do if they didn't let us thru? It was upwind from Panama to anywhere else in the Caribbean. Nevertheless we carried on. It was a good trip. Just one day to weather and the rest of the trip the wind was free so we made good time.

In Panama the Canal authorities didn't want to let us through. We could get a tug to tow us through for 10,000 dollars or we could go around the Horn. There was no other option. With much persistence we finally got to see the Commandant. We plopped Falcon up on his desk which Falcon loved. Lots of things to throw overboard! The Commandant, while talking to us about how he couldn't do anything, kept getting his attention diverted to see what Falcon was playing with next. He only held out for 20 minutes from the full force of Karen's charm until he allowed that we could be towed through by another yacht and even that Falcon at a year and a half could count as a line handler. (Falcon did show his strength by throwing some of the pencils across the room!) We stopped for the night in Gatun Lake as we were too slow to make it through the canal in one day and to bathe in the fresh water.

Karen finally got the chance to wash Falcon's diapers in fresh water. After a year and a half of laundering diapers in saltwater Falcon instantly got diaper rash for the first time! While Karen was still pregnant in the Med we had taken one good look at the price of paper diapers and decided that we were going to use cloth. Besides where were we going to put enough paper diapers on a 24 footer to cross the Atlantic? It worked out well. For number one I tied a clove hitch on one corner of the cloth and towed it behind the boat for an hour. For number 2 it was towed for six hours. After being towed we hung the diaper on the life rails to dry in the wind. The trick was that after it dried, the wind shook the sodium chloride from the material but not before it was bleached a pure shiny white.

It was a joy to be back in the Pacific after the windy Caribbean. We spent Christmas with a fleet of cruising boats in Gulfito, Costa Rica, including 5 French boats with kids from 1 to 9 years old, one of which was El Golea, who was our tow boat in the canal. Sailing with young children is very common among the French even given the strictness and difficulty of their school system. In grade school children attend school from 7 in the morning till 6 at night. Even with the normal 2 hour lunch that is still a lot of studying. Education is taken very seriously there. Karen was surprised that the French boats started home schooling their children at 3 ½. It made us realize we had to start thinking about the future. This honeymoon we were still on was about to crash and burn if we were not prepared for upcoming changes in Falcon's and our lives.

The Pacific side of Panama and Costa Rica is a cruising paradise. Little islands abound everywhere as do national parks. In one park we went for a hike to see what we could see. It was supposed to be famed for the number and variety of monkeys. It was a beautiful trail but not a monkey could be seen. Suddenly we heard something screaming at us from the top of a tree and then a heavy body fell from limb to limb. Squawks of indignity resounded all the way down. At the bottom after the final crash the entire forest broke into peals of monkey laughter which only increased in volume as the head monkey began his slow climb back up the tree. We left Costa Rica bound towards Mexico. This meant crossing the Gulf of Tehuantepec. This is the only low spot between the Rockies and the Andes along Central America and as you can guess, the wind likes to blow through the gap and blow hard. Very hard. Normally one follows the coast keeping 'one foot on the beach' to prevent any large seas from having the opportunity to develop. We were so far out, 250 miles, I didn't think anything could happen to us. Naturally we got into a blow and for the only time sailing around the world, we were knocked down. We lost one of our solar panels and almost lost the dinghy in an all standing gybe. We swirled around and ended up heading back to where we were coming from. Maybe the sea gods were telling us something?

At this point Falcon was in the potty training stage. We had a book, 'How to potty train your child in 24 hours.' What could be easier? I read the book first, applied the principles and sat back and waited. Nothing. Karen said,

"Mike, you are doing that all wrong, it's not working. I'll have a go if you don't mind." Karen, with her fine mind and Master's degree, read the book and followed the instructions. Nothing. Zilch. Nada. Same old, same old.

We were feeling like pretty poor parents about then or if not, then it must be the kid's fault. Maybe our kid was mentally handicapped? We dropped the book next to Falcon during his nap and went out and did some work on deck. Each of us was trying not to think of our poor brain damaged child who would never fully mature. We wondered what it would be like having an 18 year old son with a 5 year old mind. An hour later when we came below there was Falcon leafing though the book looking at the pictures. A little light must have clicked on in his head like, 'Oh, that is what they were going on about!'

And just like that, he was potty trained at 20 months. We started feeling pretty damn good about ourselves. We must be good parents after all! Thoughts of handicaps were happily abolished.

Falcon decided that he did not want to sleep when put to bed. Emphatically. He wanted to stay up. He wanted to be part of the crowd, not that he wasn't. This was a 24 foot boat after all. When he was sleeping in the forepeak his head was not more than 5 feet from me, but he was in a different room. And he would cry, and cry, and cry. We read this book that said, 'Put the kid to bed and let him cry for 15 minutes, if he is still awake after that let him get up'.

Cruising is a wonderful lifestyle. You make fast friends who share many of your interests. Often when you meet a fellow cruiser it is like meeting a long lost brother. When one boat gets in serious trouble everyone pitches in to help out. In many ways it is the perfect lifestyle. One of the drawbacks is that often you are anchored so close that everything said in the cockpit is common knowledge. Now if one has a crying child...

At least once a week we had someone stop by and ask us why we were torturing our child. Every night they heard blood curdling screams coming from our boat and were thinking of contacting the authorities. They didn't seem to believe us when we told them that they were the cries of a wild Falcon; an exhausted and frustrated wild Falcon who had two parents slowly going insane. On some hot and sticky nights the 15 minutes passed by so quickly I could have sworn, if I didn't know better, that it was less than a minute!

When we were in Puerto Plata in the Dominican Republic I was given a Bermudan sling by a fellow cruiser. It was kind-of like a Hawaiian sling but different. It had a stainless steel 'arrow' that once released, flew free. So it was shoot and chase the arrow. Shoot and chase the fish swimming away with the arrow stuck in its side. I had been told that there was a steep learning curve associated with learning to use the sling and also I had to become stronger to be able to pull back on the sling without quivering. The key was to be able to make a perfect brain shot so the fish doesn't pull your arrow under a rock and out of reach. I was also told that it was worth it in the end.

We cruised up into the Sea of Cortez (Gulf of California if you are following in an atlas) in company with some friends in equally small boats. One of them 'Watchfire' was also a Columbia but 26'. Russell was a painter and Jennifer an actress and author. They were great friends and everywhere we stopped I took out my sling and swam around shooting fish. Sorry, make that shooting at fish. The Sea in those days was absolutely filled with fish but somehow I always seemed to miss them. I would love to write that I supplied fish for everyone. The best that I can do is assure you, faithful readers, that it was very good exercise.

Sailing Heaven

Educational Experience

Falcon joins a Crèche

North of La Paz, in the Sea of Cortez lies an isolated outcrop of rocks called Isla Islote. It is a beautiful island eroded by the sea so thoroughly that one can see daylight on the other side through the living rock. One day when Falcon was 3 we decided to swim around the island. We put a life jacket on Falcon much to his disgust and he hung on to his kick board. We all had our masks and fins on and the water was crystal clear. We watched fish darting this way and that on the sea bottom 70 feet below us. On the far side of the island we came upon a sea lion rookery.

It wasn't on a beach. There were no beaches, just rocks. Next to the steep cliff of the island was a shallower area that was ringed by boulders. As we approached, the big bulls swam up to me and blew bubbles in my face! It wasn't till years later I found out that this was a threat display. Back then, I found it totally charming. But either way I couldn't get any closer to the rocks. Every time I tried a big bull would get in my way. Karen was allowed to swim up to the rocks where the other mothers sat keeping a close eye on their offspring but she wasn't allowed to go into the shallow pond where the newborn pups played. Every time she tried, she received growls and an impressive display of teeth. Falcon however swam right into the pond without a glance from the guardians. He sat in the shallow water and splashed and clapped at the baby pups' antics. The mothers somehow knew that he was a pup too. We stayed for 30 minutes till we got too cold but the memories of that day will remain with us always.

_/) _/) _/)

I organized a couple of deliveries up to California from La Paz. The question was who would be crew. Normally it wouldn't be a question, Karen would go. But she was still breast feeding Falcon. Finally she said,

"Listen, Mike. Normal people take their kids wherever they go. Maybe I should make a papoose to carry Falcon on my back. The thing is Falcon and I are going on your deliveries. Period." I think I mentioned about the success of my marriage is based on not messing with The Karen? She is so easy going that on the rare exceptions when she does put her foot down it is simpler to agree.

I have always loved the wild and rough Pacific side of the Baja peninsula where the wind almost always blows out of the north. After the Red Sea, the trips to weather didn't hold much to surprise us. Falcon didn't seem to mind the change of venue. Or rather we were his world. And he, ours.

Ever since we took that knockdown in Tehuantepec I had not felt 100% about Tola. I felt she might have broken her back, strained her keel, in the knockdown, and I had been thinking about what boat we might get next and

73

where we might sell Tola. When I first brought the subject up Karen was suddenly and adamantly against any talk of selling her little boat.

"There is no way you are going to sell this boat; there is no way I am going to let you. Period!" That lasted for a while then:

"Mike, listen, if you paint the salon floor and fix that one leaky port light I will go around the world with you again in Tola. Please, don't sell my boat, Mike. Please." I didn't know why she was so adamant. Surely she could see her child growing and knew he wasn't going to suddenly stop. To change the subject I started talking about going to Hawaii next. Karen was a little suspicious as I had talked about the selling of Déjà Vu in Hilo, but Hawaii was a strong lure and off we went in November. Maybe she feared that her 3 year long honeymoon would finally be over if I sold her magic carpet.

We left Cabo San Lucas in November bound towards Hawaii. The first day out is always a transition day. It was my watch and on watch I have always held that an alert crew is better than a bored crew with glassy eyes. I feel it is better to keep active. Walk around the boat, find gear that is coming loose, don't just stand there and stare at the horizon. But that first day I wish I had. I was coming back on deck after jamming a particularly noisy mayonnaise jar into place and found we were going through a wake; a big wake. There was no ship anywhere on the horizon but it was a fresh wake. I shivered in my bones. That ship must have been doing well over thirty knots. That would be a bad time to have a collision at sea, as if anytime ever is. There would be little left of poor little Tola. I got little sleep that voyage for I kept such a good watch, often coming up on Karen's watch too just because I thought I heard something.

The rest of the trip was uneventful until we approached Hilo on the big island of Hawaii in rain and heavy squalls 24 days after leaving Cabo. The big island is always difficult to see from the windward side and it was no different this time. This was my fourth time to sail into Hilo and Tola's second. It was by far the worse approach I have ever made anywhere. If I didn't know the port so well I would have turned back to sea no matter what the weather, especially remembering our near disaster in the Red Sea.

While I stood at the helm Karen tried to see anything she could from the bow. To starboard we could hear surf crashing on a beach even above the whine of 25 to 30 knots of wind. To port huge breakers were smashing into the 2 mile long, 30 foot tall breakwater protecting the port. All around us was nonstop rain. No, that isn't right. All around us the ocean had come up and engulfed us. I could barely see Karen 15 feet away. When the surf became too loud we gybed to port and when the breakers became overwhelming we gybed back to starboard. I stopped mumbling about where my engine was and started wondering about what had happened to my radar.

Falcon was down below screaming his head off that he wanted to be on deck. The problem was I was worried that the waves, which were sweeping the boat, would get even larger as we approached the shallower water by the entrance and that if we were swept while his little body was on deck the force of the waves would crush his body against the harness and tether and all we would get back would be a body for a funeral. He had to stay down below. There was a small crack between the companionway hatch and the boards that he had somehow hooked his fingers into. He swung there, as the boat was tossed this way and that, refusing to let go. His feet lost their purchase but still he held on with the tips of his fingers screaming his head off that he wanted his mommy. As he swung there he was airborne more often than not.

Eventually we turned the corner of the breakwater and entered calmer water. Of course as always happens as soon as we were in less danger, conditions improved. Maybe the Greeks had it right. The gods are up there playing with planet size marbles and laughing at us. We let Falcon out on deck which he enjoyed in the rain after giving us a few dirty looks. You could just hear him thinking, 'Is this little bit of rain what you locked me up for? Sissies!' We pulled into the clearance dock and Falcon's eyes instantly went straight to the playground across from the customs office. As soon as all the Customs and Immigration paperwork was done he was off the boat like a dart running to the playground. Well, almost. The poor kid had forgotten how to walk without the boat moving. He was land sick after 24 days at sea. His feet were moving, it was just that he would topple onto his side while still running his damnest. We didn't help his future mental health by laughing our heads off, the poor little kid.

It happens to me too, at times. The motion of the boat becomes so normal that when I lose my balance and start to fall over, I ignore the feeling and just wait for the boat to tip back under my feet. On dry land I have a terrible time. I drive Karen crazy by tacking back and forth across the sidewalk as I walk down it. I will trip over a leaf as I have gotten into the habit of keeping my feet close to the deck in case of a bigger than normal wave comes along. It is really embarrassing especially when people laugh at me. At least I knew how Falcon felt.

It didn't take Falcon long to get his land legs back as we traveled through the islands, to get used to the transition back and forth from land to the sea. It struck me, watching his efforts, that transition is what education and life, for that matter, were all about. We were used to transits, going from one spot to another across a piece of water. But equally well, transits were also used in the logic learned in algebra to develop a business plan or a way to circumvent a fellow employee. Using the memory developed by cramming for a history test, holding a lot of different facts in your brain at the same time, was also essential to develop a Unified Theory of How to Get Ahead in Life. Karen was going to have to transit from living on Tola to living in a house to living on a new boat and it wasn't going to be easy for her. Already she was starting to cry. She ended up crying herself to sleep for two years after I sold Tola. God, she loved that boat!

We had trouble selling her. In her brief seven year cruising career Tola developed a bit of a following so after one advert three people were suing each other and me for the right to buy the boat! I ended up selling her to an Indiana Jones type character that needed her to live close to all of his different digs in the Islands. We packed all of our belongings and flew off to San Diego where we were to watch my parent's house for a few months. It was a sad moment as we turned back for the last look at the little boat that had taken us so far with so much style. I hoped that Karen remembered to pack the love we shared for so many years. I hoped we would still be on our honeymoon without our brave little boat.

Tola Hauled out in Pine Island

TRANSITION

It was a different life ashore. My parent's house was beautiful and roomy with extensive gardens. Falcon spent the first week following his mother around afraid that he would lose her. For the first part of his life he was always within sound of her breathing, now she kept disappearing out of sight into other rooms and floors. At least the house was on an island, Coronado, so some of his life was the same.

Coronado forms the seaward side of San Diego harbor. I was born here, 'on the runway', as they said in those days. It was in a clinic which was later torn down to build a runway for the North Island Naval Air Station which forms more of San Diego Harbor. All these islands used to be actual islands until a treaty with Mexico, years ago, declared all islands, south of such and such a latitude, would belong to Mexico. Overnight property owners filled in the channels between the islands to remain American.

Falcon couldn't understand our fascination with television. For us it was a return to our youth; for Falcon it was boring. We built him a two story fort with a sandbox on the bottom in the back yard and he didn't understand why we weren't out there playing with him all day long. By the time we arrived, Coronado was no longer a Navy family island, like it was when I was young, but was now a retiree and wealthy resort island. There were few kids Falcon's age to play with, but then that was his life as an only child.

Karen wanted to go to her sister's wedding and to earn the plane fare she became a crossing guard for a few hours a day. At first she kept Falcon with her in his stroller but soon she met a day care owner who was impressed with the nerve and élan with which Karen stopped eighteen year old sailors just off the farm speeding down the street, and volunteered to watch Falcon for free. No crying this time. I think he was disappointed with our TV watching!

I was driving a small passenger ferry and running my own company called 'Husband for Rent.' It was a real money maker. I catered to widows and working couples who needed a man around for an hour a day just to do all those difficult guy things. I got a lot of grief from family and friends that I was selling my body but surprisingly I never had any requests. Maybe I should have been concerned?

We spent many happy hours boat looking. San Diego was full of boats. We discovered a surprising number were selling for less than 20 thousand dollars when we put more than a casual effort into our search. One a 57' ferrocement ketch, which didn't look all that bad, was offered at 15 thousand. Karen liked it because of a walk in refrigerator. I could only imagine the power needed to keep it cold! We opened negotiations on a couple boats to test the depth of the water and discovered the asking price was amendable. We almost bought a 35' ketch but there was trouble with the paperwork.

My father had bought a boat, years ago, and sold it after playing with it for a few years. He kept the paper and the new owner financed with him a low monthly payment and a balloon payment which 8 years later the buyer couldn't make. The new owner had been trying to sell her halfheartedly which doesn't work in Southern Cal. All the boats for sale there are beautiful works of art. The competition is fierce. Anyway I repossessed the boat and as payment my Dad sold the boat to me. Or maybe it was just to get his house back from his guests! She was a Dickerson 41 ketch, an East Coast boat, shoal draft, full keel, teak deck and fiberglass hull.

Years ago I single-handed a 28 foot woody, 'Déjà Vu', from San Diego to Hawaii. I was 20 and should have known better than to head off shore in an unproven boat. It was a classic young man's voyage. I had a sextant, a book on how to navigate, a stop watch and an am/fm radio. I picked up am radio stations at night. When they told the time on the hour I started my stop watch to figure out GMT hours later for my noon sight. The trip took 40 days mostly because I was so cold that I headed due south to warm up. That got me down into the hurricane season which was exciting. The crux of the matter was, after 40 days at sea, the teak deck was opening up and I could see sunlight through some of the seams. That was fine while it was sunny. It was less fun during squalls when all my bedding and clothes got wet. After that experience I swore that I would never own another boat with a teak deck. And yet here I was, with another! Part of the reason was the boat was really trashed and my Dad would have had to put a fortune into her to get a good price and he was offering it to me, in turn, at a great price. She was a big ketch with lots of room for a growing boy. She was called 'Beau Soleil' or 'Beautiful Sun' in French which was close enough to 'beautiful son' for me. Maybe it was for my father also? Naw, not a prayer!

After we fixed the motor and repaired the worse of the rigging problems we took her for a day sail to see what we had exactly, sailing wise. We knew we were spoiled by the sailing perfection of engineless Tola, but we hoped our boat wouldn't be too clunky. We gave Falcon the helm for part of the day. He was only 3½ but he had been sailing for all of that so we were surprised every time he had the helm, he headed for the shore. I put my hands on the wheel next to his to guide her back on a course down the bay. After three times of heading for the shore I finally asked why he was going that way.

"Going to the beach, Dad." Well, of course. I should have known. That's what boats are for after all, going to exotic beaches around the world.

One of the great things about Coronado was the garage sales every Thursday morning. More of a social event than a way of supplementing income it was a great way to get together. Everyone rode bikes so we got our exercise too. After a year of collecting goodies it became your turn to clean house and have a garage sale. With an empty boat we enjoyed the great prices to the utmost. The best things we bought were hand puppets and Lego. The puppets became Falcon's guide through his more difficult roadblocks. We reached these difficult times when we wanted to do one thing, for Falcon to try to read for example, and he wanted another, to play on the beach until midnight, then out would come the puppets. One puppet would take our position and another would be the devil's advocate. Our little passion play would go something like this:

"I'm going to go to the beach and build a sand castle. No, I'm going to build a hundred sand castles and then I'm going to knock them all down. And then I'm going to build them again. So there. And you can't stop me."

The next puppet would say, "But what if you get sun burned? That really hurts. I got sun burnt one time and I had to sleep standing up it hurt so much! Know what the bad part was? My Mommy told me to come in but I didn't listen. I didn't want to. But later when I couldn't sleep I wished I had listened to her." All delivered in a high kid's voice, of course. Or, Fast Freddy, one of his favorites, would say,

"I wish someone would read me a book. One day I am going to be able to read books all by myself. Then I'm going to read books all the time whenever I want to, even in Falcon's tree fort and no one can stop me!"

I think the reason the puppets worked was it separated the argument from the personal power struggle. Seeing the argument standing alone he could appreciate the logic of our position.

Falcon had trouble with pronouncing f. We named two of his favorite 'buddies' with f's in their names. Besides 'Fast Freddy' there was 'Fearless Feline." Little did we know that f is the last letter children learn to pronounce. All that parental angst wasted!

The Coast Guard was very determined to fine the parents of children who were not wearing life jackets in dinghies. I really couldn't argue especially given how cold the water was in winter. Falcon resented the entire life jacket scenario. He fought putting the jacket on, he fought taking it off, he fought everything to do with life jackets. Karen solved it by making a little life jacket for Falcon's favorite stuffed animal. 'Tugs' had to wear his jacket also whenever he went into the dinghy, and Falcon had to put it on him.

One struggle we had, I lost. We went to a garage sale with Falcon riding on the kid's seat on his mother's bike. One guy was selling stuffed animals. Falcon instantly fell in love with a huge camel which was as big as he. The guy started at $5, which was a relief as Falcon only had a dollar he had earned killing flies. Slowly Falcon bargained the man down over the 20 minutes we were there. In the end he got his camel for 5 cents. Over the next 15 years I tried to talk Falcon into throwing away his camel or at least selling or giving it to someone as it took up a third of his berth. The silly camel is still there today even though Falcon is off in San Diego at college. Slowly over the years I appreciated the position the guy was in who sold Falcon the camel. He wanted it out of his house in the worse way!

In many major department stores we found loads of educational materials for pre-school through third grade. Given this wealth of material we didn't worry about home schooling. What could be easier? Oh, how the ignorant walk into the lion's den!

We finally got Falcon to sit down and watch Sesame Street. I was a great fan and considered Count Dracula as one of the great American heroes of our generation. Falcon was totally bored. We could bribe him with cookies to sit and watch but as soon as they were gone he was up and out the door. We definitely had bred an outside type of kid.

In August, for Falcon's birthday, we drove up to Whidbey Island in Puget Sound to visit my parents in their summer home. We stayed for 2 weeks and I was surprised at their friends who came to visit. Instead of just sitting around during the day, they all found a job to do. They didn't ask for directions or suggestions or permissions. They saw something that had to be done and went out and did it. My parent's generation, or at least the Navy subsection of it, is really the gung ho generation.

Karen during this time was still crying at night and blaming me for selling Tola. When we moved on to 'Beau Soleil' in late October the crying got worse. It was cold and foggy. The boat was new to us and half of its equipment still didn't work. The stove was kerosene and both didn't work well and was smelly. The heads had passed the point of no return. Mildew had invaded and declared victory. Dry rot permeated the boat. Karen tried to put a brave face on and to do her best. It was a hell of an uphill battle. It was not the beautiful tropics where we were used to sailing. After a hard day's work, she couldn't jump overboard for a swim; at least not without freezing to death. She was so homesick for the life on Tola I had taken from her. And she blamed me for it. She was sure I was selling my body while at work. Our honeymoon was starting to go on the skids.

For me the good part of living on the boat was I could get a lot more done. If I had a spare 20 minutes at the house I would most likely turn on the boob tube, as it was not enough time to even get to the boat much less do something. But living on her, in 20 minutes I could solve a small problem. The bad part was little things become huge when a girl is not happy. Everything had to stop while the trauma was solved. I was determined to get the boat ready to leave for the south and far horizons. Falcon and I wanted our Karen back!

One of the major problems was the roller furler on the jib. In any kind of wind at all it could not be furled. The bearings were gone, not broken, missing! I became a dealer for Pro Furl to get a discount on a unit.

It was a little dishonest. I didn't intend to ever sell any others. I pacified my conscience by telling it that this was business as usual. I don't think it believed me!

We could have spent years getting the boat ready to go cruising. I was determined not to. I enjoy working on my boat in foreign ports. One of the big selling points for Tola was the many different types of wood in her cabin. Each was bought in a different country and each had its own story to tell. These days most boat parts are available world wide. The more difficult to find can always be bought when returning to the US for Christmas or birthdays.

Falcon loved moving on to the boat. He returned to a life he understood. Plus, because of power constraints we stopped bugging him about educational television. Instead he had us read to him. He felt so at home in the forepeak of Beau as he had on Tola. It was like a little cave that he could snuggle in. I would have worried about him withdrawing from the world and into the world of books if he wasn't such an outside type of guy. Any chance he had, we were encouraged to be climbing the mast or playing in the playground with him.

"Dad, I've got a great idea! Let's go over to the park and build a fort in the sand while Mom is making breakfast!"

"But Falcon, breakfast will be ready in just a few minutes."

"Well, we better hurry up and go then or our oatmeal will be cold when we get back!"

We could dinghy from the boat to shore and land on a beach, a big plus in the kid department. Next to the beach was a playground with a sandbox. Falcon thought his boat was perfect and anchored in a perfect place. From living in a hell where he could never find his mother he moved back to a life he understood. Karen liked rowing me ashore in my captain's uniform complete with four stripes and scrambled eggs on the hat. It made her feel important but it got me into a lot of trouble.

One of the big events in Coronado is the Friends of the Library's book sale. It relies on donations. Coronado is so affluent that the quality of the books was very high. We needed a good atlas, dictionary and a variety of educational books. The book sale was the perfect place to get them for a very good price. So there I was at the book sale, in my stripes and cap, as I was driving the ferry just after the sale, bargaining hard like the sailor I was and everyone was looking at me wondering how a Captain in the Navy (the uniforms are almost identical) ever got to be such a tight wad! We were supposed to be helping the library, not bargaining all the profit out of the sale! I wasn't aware of the feeling until I turned around and saw the faces. These were the people my parents had to live with everyday and in a way were my employers; they all knew who I and my parents were. Oops, screwed up again! At least we got to sail away, eventually.

It was a happy and a sad day when we departed Coronado. Happy because we were off on another adventure, sad, because Coronado and San Diego are very special places. Falcon and I had been very happy there, Karen had too in a way. She really liked working in the garden and having a full kitchen to mess about in. She still resented losing her Tola but I hoped to convince her that she now had a bigger, fancier carpet for a new wonderful life. And that the magic was always hers to have, she just had to click her heels.

Painting Tola on the Sand Bar in Hawaii

CHILDHOOD

Nine months after we sold Tola, we moved on board Beau Soleil and fifteen months AT (after Tola) we set sail south towards the Sea of Cortez, Mexico. It was great to be underway again even with the continuing problems we had with the boat. That is nothing against our boat. Any boat heading out to sea after a prolonged stay in port develops a myriad of problems. It's almost like our boat was getting seasick! But we were sailing towards our dream again.

Fellow Adventurer and faithful reader, you might wonder why I am always saying, 'towards' instead of 'to'. It might seem just a little thing but it is not. To go 'to' a place is to say, 'that is where I am going.' It is to say, 'It doesn't matter what the weather is, that is where I am going. It doesn't matter even if a hurricane is brewing, my mind is made up.'

Instead, we say we are heading 'towards' a place, recognizing that we exist on the ocean not because we can master its strength, but because we are really good at side stepping its blows. When the ocean decides no one is sailing in that direction today, it is the wise sailor who recognizes a force greater than his own and goes somewhere else. We say things like:

'OUR PLANS ARE SET FIRMLY in jello.'

'NO MATTER WHAT, WE ARE DEFINITELY, thinking about, LEAVING TODAY!'

'OUR MINDS ARE SET. WE ARE LEAVING TODAY or the next, or the next, or DEFINITELY one day soon.'

It is a mindset embraced by a whole breed of sailors. It is into this life and philosophy that Falcon was immersed as he grew up. So we can't blame him about how it all ended up. He was doing as he was taught, by example. But, my, I am getting ahead of Falcon's educational explanation, aren't I?

We had great fun stocking up the boat. We started just after we painted all the lockers inside and out. We were lucky enough to have found a Canned Goods store 10 miles from the boat. This store sold brands of food that didn't make it in our big competitive world. These were brands that couldn't afford the advertising to become household names. Eventually they go bankrupt and stores like Canned Goods buy out all their leftover product. It was really great fun. We bought one of each item we were interested in and returning to the car, we had a gigantic picnic trying them out. Falcon loved it. If we all agreed, including Falcon, that the contents were good, we would buy a case or two. Undented 16 ounce cans usually sold for 5 to 7 for a dollar in 1992.

Every morning I would peruse the 'Thrifties' in the newspaper for marine items. At times we would make wild dashes around San Diego buying stoves and anchors and the like for pennies on the dollar. For Falcon it was a great adventure with his parents, for me it was like spear fishing, the hunt and the kill, for Karen it was time away from the boat she still resented. She worked as hard or harder than any of us getting the boat ready, I want that to be very clear. Karen is a seriously hard worker. The better the boat looked and worked, the less sad she became. She particularly resented the kerosene stove the boat came with. We visited a RV outlet store and picked up three RV propane stoves for free from a pile in the back. There were hundreds waiting for the junker. I cannibalized the three and with our kerosene stainless shell from the boat created a Frankenstein like cooker. This lasted for 12 years till its macabre birth led to its physical destruction in a puff of smoke and I had to replace it.

It must have been something he learned in day care. Falcon started crying and having a fit whenever he wanted something. The battle of wills that developed eventually settled around Frosted Flakes. Falcon really wanted his favorite cereal and his Mother was equally determined that he would eat non-sugared Cheerios. From a battle of wills it deteriorated into an all out war. I was finally able to break the stalemate by remembering what a counselor did in a halfway house I was in once. It was his job to tell us, we couldn't do whatever it was that we wanted to do. Some cons would really get going and cry that their life would be ruined even more if they couldn't spend the night ashore or whatever it was they wanted. The counselor would burst into fake tears right with them saying how much he wanted to help them but he just couldn't.

We tried the same thing with Falcon. When he put on his act to get his Frosted Flakes, Karen would start crying. She told him between tears,

"I really want some Frosted Flakes, too. You know if I had Frosted Flakes right now, I would eat a 100 bowls of them. No, I would eat a 1000 bowls before I was filled up. I wish I could give you some Frosted Flakes but I don't have any. I've got an idea. Would a bowl of Cheerios do instead?" I think this worked because Karen behaved so unlike her normal self that it was funny. Humor has tamed many a wild and wily beast.

Underway Karen was still sniffling about the selling of Tola, all the way down the Baja coast. I did notice that there was starting to be a lack of conviction to it. Falcon was in seventh heaven on board the boat. He had his Mom back; he always knew where she was and he had both of his parents always on call to tell stories to him and read him books. About halfway down the Baja it started to get warm and we met some old friends at sea on 'Nalu IV' heading north after completing their circumnavigation. Karen's sniffles suddenly dried up.

Baja is a beautiful place, as long you like the dry chaparral desert landscape. Even if it you don't it will grow on you. But as magnificent as the scenery is, the true beauty of Baja is the people. I was very happy years later when NAFTA came out as Mexico has so much that we as Americans lack. What, dear reader, you are surprised? What does Mexico have that we don't?

I think primarily, as a new father back then, the love for and care of children struck me as different south of the border. All children were cared for not just their own. It was a truism that if you accidentally ran over a kid, who are always running and playing in the street, the best thing to do is to pull the car over and shoot yourself in the head as that is nothing compared to what the crowd will do to you. There was no abuse of children, if you ignore child labor, in Mexico.

The Mexican government subsidized the cost of basics for its citizens. Bread, tortillas, and toothpaste were the three most common. Much better than the American habit of subsidizing General Motors and Delta! Once I went down to San Felipe, at the head of the Sea of Cortez, to capture some dolphins for a marine park in San Diego. In applying for the permits we were prepared to pay a mordita, a bribe, literally 'a little death'. It is the way of doing business in Mexico and we were prepared to drop considerable monies into various officials' pockets. Imagine our surprise when the mordita turned out to be to build an aquarium for the University of Guadalajara. Instead of enriching themselves, the officials thought of their country first. How many American officials can say the same?

Mostly what really separates Mexico from America is the American custom of dealing with business as quickly as possible compared with a Mexican's habit of prolonging every transaction in an attempt to extract every ounce of pleasure possible. It seems a small difference. Your average American is busy trying to get somewhere else as fast as possible while your average Mexican is very happy just where he is. Mexico is a very relaxing place to live.

We took this lesson to heart and now as we go around the world and people ask us where our favorite spot is in the whole world, we always answer with the name of the island or town where we are then anchored. When asked why, we reply 'what good is it to wish you are somewhere else? Enjoy to the utmost where you are. Instead of resenting you are here rather than some where else, grasp the most joy you can out of where you find yourself, today.' As some song writer said, "If you can't be with the one you love, love the one you are with."

We loved to read to Falcon. Long before he was born, we used to read to each other. Crossing the Indian on Tola, we read 'The Crystal Cave' about Merlin and Arthur growing up, aloud to each other. It seemed very natural to read to Falcon. Our choice of reading material became simpler but Falcon more than made up for that with his enthusiastic enjoyment of our efforts.

We became used bookstore patrons to satisfy Falcon's addiction. That is unfair. We enjoyed the reading just as much as Falcon. Still he liked to tell and hear stories more.

An old Hawaiian game is 'Talk Story' in which the objective is to get the next teller of the story in so much trouble he gets stuck, gets flustered and gives up. It works like this. The first person starts the story and gets the hero into as much trouble as he can and just as it is getting impossible to solve he calls out another person's name. The next person can take the story in any direction he wishes and as he builds the story, he passes it on to the next person. Sounds simple? It is anything but! We played this one night on the beach in Bora Bora with a bunch of cruisers after a potluck. Many of them, years later, wrote back to us saying that night was the high point of their circumnavigation. It did help that Falcon, 9, was a pro at the game and kept the ball rolling. Certainly it aided his ability to speak and think on his feet and his growing imagination.

The kid's greatest passion became fishing. On Tola this involved towing a line behind our rowing dinghy. Sometimes he didn't have bait on it but he didn't seem to mind. It was the fishing that mattered. Well, that goes for a lot of us grown up fishermen too!

Now, on Beau Soleil, we caught a lot of fish and Falcon loved to help if only to get in the way. When I cleaned the fish, we looked through the organs and identified one or two for each fish. He really liked looking down their mouths. Maybe he was waiting for them to talk to him!

The Pacific side of the Baja Peninsula is very rugged and with the exception of a couple towns and Ensenada, it is inhabited only by fishing camps. Years ago I always stocked up with trading goods before going to these fishing camps. Now Karen was restricting my trade. She put her foot down. She wasn't going to stand by and watch me poison poor defenseless fishermen by trading with alcohol and tobacco. I didn't complain too much lest she started to restrict my habits! The fishermen really wanted 22 shells and would trade a lobster for one shell; however the Mexican secret police took a dim view of supplying arms to 'potential revolutionaries'. The prison term for arms dealing was 20 years which in a Mexican jail was essentially a life sentence as no one can live that long. You would be happier in hell.

So for trading, Karen brought babies' and children's clothes from the garage sales on Coronado. I looked at her like she was crazy but the fishermen went wild! We had so many lobsters! In retrospect I saw the logic in Karen's plan. Away from their families for 3 months at a time, they became very homesick and wanted anything that would bring their families closer in their minds. They could imagine the joy on their kid's faces as Dad returned home bearing gifts.

When we arrived in Cabo San Lucas we were fat and sassy and we didn't even stop and eat at the Broken Surfboard, one of my old haunts from my days cruising these waters aboard Tola before I went west about. Cabo had really changed. Moorings were everywhere. No longer could we anchor in front of the Hacienda and enjoy the many beauties swimming out half naked to the boat. Wait, wait. I was a married man now. Maybe it was better that we had to anchor way out in the boonies! The beach was just as beautiful with pure white sand which Falcon totally loved. Karen was living in bliss. She could count the grains of sand under the boat in the crystal clear water and sunbathe topless on her boat in the tropical sun. Long gone was the sad little girl of San Diego. The girl I married was back again. Yaaaaahay!

On the beach, wandering salesmen abound. They had everything from toys to art to clothes. The toy salesmen saw Falcon and were certain they had a guaranteed sale. No such luck. When they put a toy into Falcon's hands, they expected us to buy it rather than chance a temper tantrum. Instead, we let him play with it to his hearts content. In the way of children, he tired of it within ten minutes or so and wanted something else. On the beach, we were in no hurry. If the salesman wanted to amuse our kid for an hour, fine! It was good training for Falcon. He learned that it is not the owning of a thing that makes it desirable, and that desire at first glance is a poor indicator of future happiness.

After a couple of days in tourist land, we headed up the coast towards La Paz. This is a fairyland world with few boats, lots of fish and wild lonely beaches. We spent our days making love, walking along lonely deserted beaches, making millions of sand castles and, of course, working on the boat. We could have stayed in San Diego until the boat was all fixed up but what fun would that be? Here we were in one of the most beautiful spots in the world making our boat into the dream yacht we always wanted and, when we were finished for the day, we dove in and swam naked in the beautiful crystal waters of the Sea of Cortez. How could life be better?

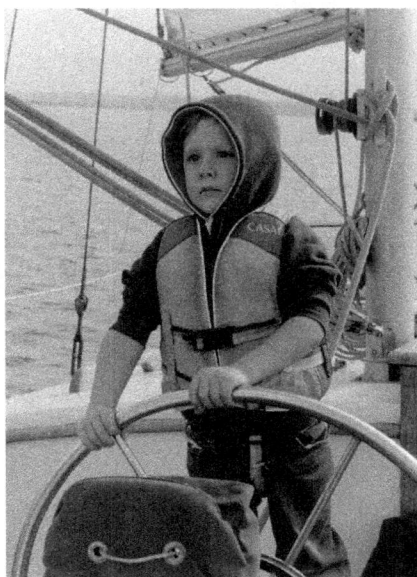

Falcon Looking For the Beach

Educational Experience

Sammy

In Aqua Verde, Mexico, we woke up one morning to find a sea lion sleeping in our dinghy. My first thought was, 'yuck', as the animal had been sick and the entire boat was filthy. Luckily, my second thought was to call 4 year old Falcon to come look, as this would be a great biology lesson. On closer examination, we discovered that the poor mammal had a fishing net so stuck over his head that it had sunk, not only into his fur, but also into his flesh.

"We have to save him, Dad!" was the excited comment. But as soon as we approached the injured sea lion, it jumped into the water and swam away. We spent the day cleaning the dinghy and listening to Falcon jabber away about how close he got to the sea lion. The next morning the animal was back sleeping in the dinghy. After a long lecture about how fast sea lions are out of the water and how sharp their teeth were I let Falcon try to approach the animal. I even went so far as to show him my old scars from sea lion bites that he had seen many times before. Falcon got within 6 feet before the mammal swam away. Again he left us a pile of runny feces and tears, tears were running down his face, Falcon was sure, because he was so hungry. He was a very scrawny sea lion. As far as we could tell the net covered his entire face and he was unable to eat.

The other boats in the anchorage told us the same thing had happened to them and now they pulled up their dinghies to keep them clean. Then, Falcon had a great idea, "Let's keep the windsurfer in the water. It's much lower to the water, for getting in and out, and to clean it we just have to roll it over." Needless to say it was a great success and we decided to try to get the net off his face. I could get within 10 feet, Karen within 8 but within a couple of days Falcon was getting within 3 feet. He laid down on the bow of the windsurfer and, 'Sammy', as he was now known, lay on the stern. He tried to feed Sammy many times a day. He was very inventive with his recipes but nothing worked. Mostly Sammy just wanted to rest, and to get better by himself. He just needed peace and quiet. After a week, Sammy accepted Falcon as some kind of handicapped, slightly demented, baby sea lion. He tried to pull the netting off, and sun damaged, it broke into pieces. The skin had grown over the cuts the monofilament had made in his skin. Amazingly, as Sammy got better he and Falcon would paddle his windsurfer all over the bay. Well, Falcon would paddle and Sammy sun bathe. Every day Sammy would disappear for longer and longer times and come back to the boat fatter. Finally one day he didn't return. We explained to Falcon that a sea lion was a wild creature and he is happiest in the untamed ocean. It helped the sadness, a little, of losing a good and special friend.

_/) _/) _/)

To power the electric tools necessary for boat repairs, I opted out on a noisy generator and chose solar panels and an inverter instead after I learned my lesson the hard way. Or I should say Falcon learned it for me.

We were anchored in a small town further up the coast and had a gasoline powered Honda generator turned on for charging batteries. Karen and I went ashore leaving the generator running which I switched off upon returning 30 minutes later. Falcon rushed out, as normal, to see what we had bought. If the generator had been running, he wouldn't have done it but with it being quiet, he leaned his starboard leg against the muffler. It was just for a second which was long enough to leave a scar for life. The whole length of his calf was bright red and within seconds it started to bubble. Luckily we had bought ice cold beer back to the boat and cooled down the leg as much as we could. A fellow cruiser had a tube of silverdine on board which we had never heard of before but worked wonders on his burn. Another boat brought over ice, a third some cold beer for the distraught parents! All were rewarded with a certificate inducting them into the FSG and cocktails on Beau! Eventually he improved and today, at 18, he has just a faint scar, the poor abused kid.

After a lot of years gathering dust, I pulled out my Bermudian sling determined that this time I would kill fish rather than just amuse them with my inept attempts. Slowly I got better and brought back a few groupers and the rare lobster. It was a start. Swimming around was great exercise and as efficient refrigeration was rare on the Baja, spearing supplied the needed protein for Falcon without all the preservatives in canned meat. He loved swimming with me. I bought him a little spear gun that I could cock for him but it was not to his tastes. He wanted a sling like his old man. Karen took over his spear gun but didn't have any more luck than he had. The problem was there was a click when the trigger was pulled which scattered the fish which I am sure had been hunted many times before. On the other hand the sling was totally silent which made it very lethal. The other advantage the sling had was range. Since the arrow was free flying the effective range was determined by your strength not preset by the trailing string. The bad part was finding the arrow after it sailed into seaweed or deep water.

As I mentioned, the learning curve for a Bermuda sling is very steep indeed and now my son had to go through it when he borrowed my sling to have a go. I tried not to give too much advice. I knew from experience it doesn't help. For some things in life you just have to keep on banging away at it till you get better; it is easy to say but also is very hard to hear for anyone, but especially for a 4 year old. It is tough, growing up.

A Four year old is also a handful. Karen came to me in tears one afternoon.

"He is just so much work. I never get a rest. It is always 'Mom, I need this' or 'Mom, I need some help.' When will it ever end?" There were a lot of answers to that. No answer I could think of would help except one.

"Karen, come with me for a walk." Together we rowed ashore and I led her up a hill with a good view to the west. She continually asked me where we were going. I just answered,

"Come."

As we made it to the top it was getting dark. We sat down on a boulder and waited. Soon the sunset started to paint itself in beautiful and continually changing colors. It was a good one. I pointed out the colors all around us.

"Look." As the last tint of color faded into night I looked at Karen and murmured,

"So beautiful and yet so brief."

"So what are we doing up here anyway? Yeah, it was a nice sunset but so what. Falcon will have made an incredible mess that I will have to clean up. Why are we up here?"

"Soon the sunset that is Falcon will be over. He will be gone from us to voyage on his own path. On that day you will cry your little heart out. On that day you will wail that so much of his beauty was lost to you because you only saw the one little dull color in front of you instead of his beauty all around you. He is and will be beautiful. His beauty will only be yours to see for a brief time. Then he will be gone. And he won't come back every night at dusk." Karen stared at me her eyes filling with tears. Silently we returned to the boat.

For 30 minutes every day, Karen held school. They practiced handwriting and counting numbers. Afterwards, they colored everything they worked on to make it special. She is such a natural teacher. She has this attitude that says to her students, 'show me what you can do.' And they did. As her students did in Rabaul, Falcon did also.

I was very surprised that all the home schooling books emphasized the idea of non-teachers playing a major role in the student's lessons. How could I do a better job than Karen? She was so competent. I spent more time in the fun department. I elected myself recess teacher. Why not? Recess had been my favorite class in grade school! We threw a lot of balls, arranged hermit crab races, climbed to the highest peak on whatever island we were on and grunted about how beautiful it all looked with our boat anchored in the bay. Falcon thrived. It was such a pleasure to be with him. How boring it would be if I was working full time for a living and missed seeing and guiding my son as he grew up.

Friends and parties were a major component of our time in the Sea. Cruising is such a social lifestyle. Everywhere we went we found people with the same desires and goals. Within a few hours they became lifelong friends. It was only natural to want to party with them. And party we did. How could anyone not? When we or another boat came in with a huge fish, we or they circled the anchored boats and called out,

"Party on the beach tonight, we have the fish!" Everyone would bring something for a big potluck. It is amazing, given time to relax and think, how inventive some women can be in the galley when the honor of their boat is at stake. Did we eat or what! Falcon was always in the thick of things. He became used to holding his own in adult conversation. And the adults, usually FSG members by this time, had the time to relax and to pay attention to a kid.

During the day everyone had their own pursuits. 'Watchfire' with Russell and Jennifer on board were a case in point. Russell, a very successful artist in oil, painted every day. Some of his canvases were very large and a Columbia 26 does not have a big cockpit. My favorite memory is of him continually stringing different colored bed sheets across the cockpit to change the light on his painting. Jennifer had given up an acting career for love and was also writing. She eventually started a literary magazine.

Other friends had worked for years and took an early retirement to enjoy cruising before they were too old. We all have to face facts. The future is unsure. We may live to a ripe old age or we may die next week. Really it is becoming a little like Rabaul under the volcanoes. We might as well laugh now before it is too late.

OK, ok. I can hear you from here. If everyone is on vacation, who is going to do the work in the world to earn the money to buy books like this one? True, true. Absolutely right. But. You knew there was going to be a but, didn't you? Isn't one TV enough? Wouldn't you see more of your kids with only one TV in the house, with you all sitting together in the same room? How many cars do you need? You complain about who your kids are associating with, but do you drive them there? Wouldn't you have to work less and be able to spend more time with your kids if you and yours were satisfied with less? Is less bad? Are we so caught up with keeping up with the Jones that more is virtuous? Maybe it is time to change neighbors. Maybe it is time to teach your kids that it's the pursuit of happiness not the pursuit of money. Maybe it is about living a life worth while to you. It's not about what you can sell or do or even do for your loved ones. It is about attainment. Reaching your own goals, not your boss's, and not your neighbor's. And, at the end of the day, seeing your creation grow into adulthood, and being able to see that growth because you are not working 40+ hours a week.

We watched Falcon grow bigger every day. I think he really enjoyed life because we enjoyed his successes so much. Did you ever have a friend, a really good friend who, when you told him about a success in your life, didn't look at you with envy in his eyes but pure joy? That is what we wanted to give to Falcon. Of course, we had our bad days. Who doesn't?

My worse mistake was when Falcon caught his first fish on a bare hook while I was going through the learning curve on the Bermudian sling. I have to defend myself and say it was just for a millisecond. Just before I caught myself. But just for that second, just for that millisecond, I felt jealous. I hope to God that it didn't translate to my eyes and if it did, Falcon didn't pick up on it. I cursed myself that night. I sat in the cockpit cursing myself for not being worthy of such a great kid, for potentially sowing the seeds that could lead to his downfall. I promised myself I would be a better dad, no; I would be a better man.

Falcon and Sammy

Educational Experience

Fishing

Falcon loves everything to do about fishing. He loves the fight to get the fish in to the stern of the boat. He loves the teamwork to gaff and land the fish. He loves the making of the lures to hook the fish. He loves the killing and eating. He loves the talking about it afterwards, often endlessly. He didn't love the cleaning of the fish. If fact he refused to have anything to do with it. It was left for me to do.

I didn't think that was fair. Why should I have to clean his fish when most often I would have been just as happy with something to eat from our well supplied lockers? Years ago, when Karen first moved on board I taught her the three C's. The three C's are to Catch, Clean, and Cook your own fish. I decided that it was Falcon's turn to learn this when he turned 7.

Dear Reader and Fellow Fish Cleaner, I am sure you have heard of the ultimate hurricane and the boat anchored in the world's perfect anchorage, which would win? That was nothing compared to the challenge of getting Falcon to stick his hands into the guts of a fish. I tried everything. I ate the raw still quivering fish, we decided that Falcon should study Biology and dissect a fish instead of a frog, he wasn't allowed to fish unless he agreed to clean his catch. Nothing worked. He ate the quivering fish alive with relish as long as I passed it to him, he was glad to study Biology as long as I did the cutting and he out lasted us on the moratorium on fishing. He quite happily sat down below making lures at all hours of the day and ignored the stern of the boat till we were too hungry for fresh fish not to let him go back to work. The thing was that Falcon was really good at catching fish. I think his record was 22 fish, over 10 pounds, in 30 minutes. I don't know how the kid did it. Maybe it had something to do with not touching fish guts? NO, NO, NO! NO, WAY!! This was one of those parenting moments where the future was to be determined. Was Falcon going to rule the roost or I?

Falcon was determined. He was always determined in anything to do with fishing. When he was 2 in the Sea of Cortez, he insisted on dragging a line with a little hook on it whenever we went anywhere in the dinghy. No bait on it, just a bare hook. We tried to talk him into putting bait on the hook. But, no, it seemed it was fine just the way it was. We were in the Sea for six months hiding from the hurricane season and he trolled his little line every day very happily, caring little about his lack of success. Of course, all of our fellow cruisers were of little help. Our neighboring boats thought he was the cutest thing they ever saw, and encouraged him to continue his fishing.

"Don't worry; soon you will catch a whale!"

"Good luck fishing, Falcon!"

"We saw a big one following your dinghy just as you were getting close to the back of our boat!" A 2 year old will believe anything he is told as long as it isn't his father telling him! Our fellow yachties were only trying to help, but they weren't helping me. When he turned 8, I hit on a great idea. I knew how to get Falcon to clean fish.

"Falcon, I wonder if we could find out what these fish are eating. If we knew that, then you would know what colors to make your lures. Do you know what? I bet if we opened up the stomach we could see what they are eating." That went over great and he became very excited. The next fish he caught he was right in there with me as I was cleaning it.

"Dad, cut open the stomach!"

"Me? No way, that is too yucky. You do it. I'm not going to do it." This impasse lasted for two more fish till he asked me which of the guts the stomach was. I could smell victory. Within a month, he was cleaning fish with the best of them.

He eventually did catch a little 6 inch half beak with a bare hook at the age of two. If your child has a desire let him run with it. Don't break his spirit. Instead of saying 'Because I said so,' be tricky!

_/) _/) _/)

We kept heading north deeper in to the Sea of Cortez. This was hurricane season so we always kept a possible hurricane hole in mind. Falcon loved the looking for holes. We would find a likely bay and do a quick survey with the sounding lead from the dinghy. Falcon was the lead thrower. Of course the lead thrower has to count the knots as they go thru his fingers to tell the depth. You knew that, didn't you? Karen was the map maker and I the rower. Afterwards, Karen and Falcon would color the map with yellow for the beaches, red for the reefs and blue for the deep water. I wasn't allowed to color. After a few well-timed abortive attempts, Falcon told me that I didn't stay inside the lines. I wanted to give him his successes even if I had to be tricky to do it!

Of course, we had a couple of close approaches of hurricanes. Close enough to be scary but not dangerous. The way it works, is you start out sailing being frightened of a 25-knot squall. After a few of those it is old hat but a gale is still scary. After a gale or two the fear eases off but there are still hurricanes. Eventually, you go through the tornados in the eye wall of a category 5 hurricane, and while you always prepare after that kind of experience, the fear of the unknown is under control, hopefully.

After the hurricane season was over we headed south. The Mexican coast from Mazatlan to Acapulco is tourist central but it was still beautiful. The cliff divers of Acapulco were good but what was really great was the cut flower market. Four city blocks of cut flowers, fresh every day, were being bought and shipped out all over the world. The colors were incredible and the aroma, mind blowing!

This time in the Gulf of Tehuantepec, where Tola was knocked down, we went the safe way, keeping one foot on the beach all the way around the big bay. A week later as we rowed in to clear customs into Costa Rica we ran into a problem, a potentially life changing problem. The officials were very distant to start. When they saw we had a son they became worse. Eventually they told us that Karen and Falcon were to be detained while I took an examiner out to the boat.

"What are you talking about?" It was getting very weird, so weird that I didn't make a big fuss. I tried to get something out of the examiner as I rowed him out to the boat. He was very quiet and reserved, almost secretive. The fact that he came out at all says a lot, as our little rowboat was tender enough to have scared all past officials off the potentially wet ride. He came on board and took one look down below and it was as if the clouds had disappeared and the sun came out. He was all smiles and made a lark of going back to the beach. He didn't even mind when he got his beautiful brown leather shoes wet. What had been going on, he wouldn't say.   Back at the office, stern faces turned cheerful but no one was talking. Eventually Karen got a secretary to blab. The last boat to clear in was a half-sinking hulk. They had 5 children living in squalor on board, in the worse possible conditions. The officials had seized the children and put them into foster homes in Costa Rica and forced the parents to leave the country. They thought we were of the same stripe and were prepared to deal with us likewise.

We liked Costa Rica even after our stormy start. The beauty of the country was astounding. The wild life was fun. Everywhere we hiked we saw weird stuff. Falcon insisted we stop and watch leaf cutter ants, five rows across, move their nest from one tree to another. Maybe it is not just humans that try to keep up with the Jones!

In Panama there was this little island with a great beach but cliffs around the rest of the island. We decided to hike around the cliffs and somewhere along the way I said, that really, we are thousands of feet high on a mountain and if we slipped the 2 feet into the deep water at our feet, we would die a horrible death on the rocks, thousands of feet below. If only I knew what I had started; I would have never stopped at that island. I would have never stopped at Panama. We would have gone around the Horn to avoid such trouble. It is hard to believe that a little event like that at 4 years of age would have set Falcon off on a life of rock climbing.

What was that, Dear Reader? What's wrong with rock climbing, you say? Have you every seen the prices of the gear they think they need to go up a hill? But here I am calling the kettle black. Sailing isn't the cheapest sport around. We get around it by declaring our sailing, a lifestyle, not a sport. In reality we are deceiving ourselves. I guess we should be happy that he found a desire in life that doesn't involve drinking or drugs. Sorry, I am getting ahead in the story.

Transiting the canal this time was a breeze. Hey, we had a motor! Or did. 100 miles from the canal our oil cooler decided life was too cruel and laid down and died. There were lots of coolers in Panama, all for ships 100 times our size. Eventually we made our own out of a condenser from an air conditioner with suggestions from some friends.

My parents flew in to help as line handlers and we had a ball. Everything was going so well I should have known the Mexican Law of Limitations would come into play. On the Caribbean side in Cristobal, somehow I managed to fill the diesel tank with water! Fortunately we had a petcock on the bottom of the tank and as water is heavier than diesel we drained it out. Of course, I had closed the valve allowing the diesel to reach the engine and then forgot to open it again when we left the harbor. Luckily the boat wasn't near anything when the motor ran out of fuel. I don't think my parents were too impressed with me!

On the Caribbean side we stopped at the San Blas Islands. Paradise on earth! What a beautiful place and people! The Kuna Indians, the only Indians who successfully fought Cortez and his Conquistadors, live in unbelievable peace. It was interesting to expose Falcon to people like these at such an impressionable age. Karen traded for Molas, which are reverse appliqué designs the Kuna women use to decorate their clothes. Falcon and I windsurfed, beached combed, and read books. The spear fishing was poor, the Kunas had to feed themselves after all, but it was still fun trying. Time just flew by, like a summer vacation.

After a month we tore ourselves away and crossed to Cartagena. Columbia is a very dangerous country. Buses are machine-gunned while on their routes, routinely. Kidnapping is a way of life. Anyone accidentally witnessing a drug deal is summarily shot. I really don't know why anyone would go there, except for Cartagena.

Cartagena is special. In all the world it is special. This is where the drug lords send their children to go to school and their families to live. The cartels have declared it a non-combatant city. There is little sign of police or crime. Both are controlled by the cartels. Yachties have dropped their wallets on the sidewalk by accident and on retracing their steps found both their wallets and their money untouched. No one dared take a chance. The cartels don't believe in trials and lawyers.

Everyone's favorite part is the castle. It is a real castle. Even the dungeons are real, half filled with water and luckily only inhabited by rats. It took hours to explore there were so many secret hidey-holes. In town, emerald dealers were everywhere. Karen and I had fun. I bought Karen a pair of emerald earrings but not till I had received free gifts from every jeweler in town. For gifts they gave us little donkey dolls with bags of raw emeralds on either side. All our relatives got Colombian Christmas Crafts that year!

Next we went to Jamaica where we managed to get arrested. The problem was we didn't think. I didn't try to see the world through other's eyes. We arrived off Port Antonio in the middle of the night. Again we didn't have an accurate chart, so we heaved to 5 miles off the coast to wait for daylight. An hour before dawn we heard big deep engines but no running lights. We had been through this before and sure enough the Jamaican police boarded us and the entire boat was searched. After 2 hours we were escorted into their docks with armed guards on board. They must have been up most of the night as one of them let Falcon hold his rifle as he took a quick nap! Once in, we were searched again, exhaustively. They found nothing, as there was nothing to find and eventually they released us to enjoy the pleasures of the port. They were sure any boat coming from Columbia must be loaded with drugs. And they thought we stopped off shore to drop them off.

The boat boys of the port were very nice to Falcon. They took him for rides on their surfboards around the anchored boats. They taught him about the wildlife along the shore and the different types of vegetables and fruits that they were selling. I think that they were trying to make up for how mean the officials had been. Jamaica was full of really nice people. The only nasties were the tourists and the officials, as usual.

Jamaican rum is famous but far more interesting were their wines. Back then, these were for sale in small distilleries in every town. You brought your own bottle to be filled from huge vats. Our favorite by far was prune wine. It tasted really delicious. The only draw back was it had predictable consequences the next morning.

We received free passes to an all inclusive resort for the day. It was intended for families and was really nice. We were at the restaurant and 4 1/2 year old Falcon, bored, was wandering around, probably looking for the beach, when he was purposely shoved by another boy. He instantly shoved back but his balance and strength learned at sea betrayed him and the other boy went flying and started crying. Falcon sensing all the eyes in the restaurant focused on him walked up to the boy and stated in a loud voice,

"Let that be a lesson for you not to start fights." Oh, my. Karen and I looked at each other and thought at the same time, 'This kid is going to be a handful in a few years.'

In Montego Bay, Falcon finally conquered rowing the dinghy. He had been trying for ever, it seemed, to row equally with both oars in order to maintain a straight course. Being able to row the dinghy gave him unparalleled freedom. Now he could go for a row by himself to get away from his parents, to visit friends or take a walk on the beach. Really it is more than that. On a boat, everyone is so close, everyone knows exactly what everyone else is doing all the time, so much so, that everyone becomes, in a way, the same person.

Please stop, Dear Reader. I am not a communist, nor do I belong to a commune. I don't even like Kool-Aid. I am not advocating anything. I am just describing what happens when people remain very close for long periods of time. Kids don't like this. Well, they do like it in a way, as it is a very secure feeling to know exactly how the two most important people in your life are going to react. However, kids constantly try to become their own person.

Sometimes they define themselves by what they are not. 'I am not like that person,' becomes 'that person is bad. I am not like him, I'm good.'

We tried to get Falcon to define himself by his accomplishments, not by his or our lack of success. Luckily he had a lot of successes. I hope it made up for my seemly continual failures. Yeah, yeah. I can hear you. He made it around the world, etc. etc. The big things I seem to do OK on. It's the important little things I was always screwing up.

Falcon's First Fish

Educational Experience

Rowing the Dinghy

Montego Bay, on the north coast of Jamaica, was a beautiful place in those days, especially over by the yacht club along the western side of the bay.

There, I decided to teach Falcon to row.   We were in an enclosed bay with sand beaches all around; there was no way he could get into too much trouble.   The dinghy, to a young boy, is a magic carpet. Once in the dinghy, he is free. No parents to tell him what to do. No chores or school work to finish. He can be off to kill a dragon or to find a blue rose in a far off kingdom! He can be on a pirate ship, rescuing his parents from the evil side of the force, or leaving them to walk the plank, depending on how the day went! Falcon wanted to be able to go exploring in the dinghy in the worse way.

Falcon was a good rower as long as Karen or I were in the dinghy to give a little nudge on an oar this way or that, or just a verbal hint. By himself, he would slowly end up down wind and in a foul mood from frustration.

"I'll never be able to row, it's too difficult and I don't want to try anymore ever again, forever," would be his heartbreaking moan. He was making our lives miserable with his dismay. A small boat is no place to be grumpy. It is just too hard on the rest of the crew. No wonder such emphasis is made on 'laughing fellow rovers.'

To solve Falcon's problem I resorted to a trick. Secretly I tied a 50 pound test monofilament line to his dinghy's bow and convinced him to try rowing one more time. The line led to a fishing reel that we kept permanently attached to the stern pulpit with hose clamps. I let the line freewheel as he rowed this way and that. Soon he was 200 feet behind the boat and trying to row back to the boat, against the normal 20 knot trade winds, getting more and more frustrated. I called out such wonderful parenting gems such as:

"Falcon, hold both oars the same way and row them together."

"Feather your oars as you bring them back."

"You are doing great!"

"Hey, you are making it!"

Then I activated my secret (yours for only $29.99) rowing trick. Every 30 seconds, checking to make sure he wasn't looking, I would pull in some of the fishing line which would tug the dinghy's bow closer in line to Beau so he felt that he was succeeding. I could see his little face gleaming with pleasure and eyes bright with achievement as he looked over his shoulder to keep on course and to gauge his success. On finally returning to Beau Soleil I sent him down to brag to his mother as I quickly disassembled my training line. Within a week of practice he was comfortable rowing the boat without the fishing line. Success.

What did he learn? What didn't he! Practice makes perfect. Don't ever give up, keep trying. I can succeed if I try hard. I am a worthy human being.

Hopefully he didn't learn that parents can be very tricky sometimes. I felt that I might need to abuse his innocence a time or two more in the future of educating our wild Falcon!

_/)   _/)   _/)

On Grand Cayman we swam with the giant sting rays. What an experience for Falcon. We had to be careful. If you touch them on the back they involuntary attack with their tail but they love having their bellies rubbed. Falcon only lasted 15 minutes before he started to lose his nerve. Well, they were big and scary, four times his size, and he was only five!

We visited Isla Mujares in Mexico and there anchored out was Caymanifique whom we met in Greece, Malta, Canary Islands and Grand Cayman on Tola. Isobel was Falcon's godmother so we invited the two of them over for dinner. After we finished eating Falcon asked Isobel to join him on the foredeck where the two of them lay on some sail bags and gazed at the constellations. Out of the blue Falcon asked,

"Tell me about God, Isobel." She was a little taken aback and asked,

"Why do you ask me, Falcon?"

"Well, you are my Godmother!" Isobel, bless her heart, did the best she could describing God.

"God is love and He is everywhere and all you have to do is reach out and there love is."

Soon both boats were off towards Fort Jefferson in the Dry Tortugas. Dear Reader and Fellow Cartographer get out your atlases. The Florida Keys don't stop at Key West. I know that is what they tell us. It is not true. It is as far as a car will go, save for James Bond's but we are not bound by cars, are we? No, the oceans are our backyard and one of the nicest parts of that yard is the Dry Tortugas.

Dominating the island is Fort Jefferson, built during the Civil War and slowly sinking into the sea, it is cared for by a great bunch of National Park Rangers who host a blow out Thanksgiving potluck for anyone anchored off the island on that day. What a party we had!

Who knows these kinds of things happen? It does help to be lucky one day a week.

We ran up towards Venice to see Karen's parents. This time we bought bicycles instead of a car. I got a three wheeler normally used only by old people with a big basket in the stern for Falcon and the groceries. We didn't want a car as we weren't staying this time. After a month we cruised north looking for work. We found none, then headed back south, slid down to Key West and anchored behind Christmas Island.

Karen quickly found a job at an awning shop while I played at being Dad and drove a water taxi on Karen's days off. After a few months of working we tired of it. What a luxury to be able to quit whenever we felt like it! It was only possible because we had no bills. We paid no rent, generated our own electricity from the sun, caught our water from passing squalls, instead of paying for insurance we relied on our own abilities, lots of big anchors and continual vigilance. We rowed our dinghy and used bicycles for land transport. We stayed healthy through our life style and if we did get sick in the United States, we watched our back. What a racket!

While in Venice when we had passed through on Tola we visited Karen's parents one day but they weren't home. Undeterred Karen decided to make some Eggs Benedict with a hollandaise sauce packet, ham, and English muffins she had bought. We didn't buy eggs as Karen was sure her mother would have some in her refrigerator. It turned out she had only two left stuck at the end of the rack in the door of the fridge. Karen was really hungry so she had one egg and Falcon and I shared the other. It tasted really good going down but within 10 hours Falcon and I were seriously ill. We had caught salmonella poisoning.

I was sick, sure, but poor Falcon, at 14 months old, had to go to the hospital. He was still breast feeding and milk is bad, we were told, for sufferers of salmonella, so he was very sick and was withdrawn from his food supply all at the same time. The poor kid had a huge IV in his arm and had to stay in the hospital for 3 days. You can imagine the bill!

I took some Lomotil which cured me right up. Lomotil is sold in Mexico for sufferers of Montezuma's revenge but is forbidden in America as it contains trace elements of an opiate. In America we are told it is a very harsh medicine and to use it sparingly. Years later I was told by a doctor I trust, that it is exceptionally mild and I could have given it to Falcon. I mean, come on! Someone should tell our government to get a life! We are talking about people's health here!

Falcon had to stay for several days, I informed the admitting nurse that I couldn't afford the cost. She said not to worry. Imagine my concern on being presented with the bill. Not only was it huge and loaded with errors, all in the hospital's favor, it was presented by a gruff, impatient nurse with an attitude of 'pay and pay now.' Usually when someone has an attitude it is because something is going down, someone was going to be shafted; and I was afraid it was going to be me.

This wasn't my first time in an emergency room. Once in Mexico I managed some how to walk into a huge wind generator. Six inches of my scalp were torn from my head and hung on by a thin thread. At the hospital after I was sewn up, I asked the doctor how much I owed him. He replied in faultless English,

"Tip the nurse."

In Mayotte, an island in the Comorres in the middle of nowhere in the Indian Ocean, Karen needed a root canal and a new crown on a molar. There was no cost; health care was free on this island of maybe 900 people.

Falcon was never charged for any exam or inoculation anywhere around the world. Never charged in places like St. Lucia, Dominican Republic, Martinique, Panama, Australia or Fiji. He was never billed till he returned to America. Health care for children is free world wide except in 'the land of the free'.

In Australia a bloke makes a bloke's wage. Whether you are a welder or a doctor or a bus driver you are paid much the same. If you become a Doctor it is because you have a calling to heal people not because you want to get rich.

In Chagos I was bitten by one mean mother of a spider on the elbow and developed septic arthritis. I needed massive amounts of

Ciprofloxicillin if I wasn't to lose the arm. It was very scary. My upper arm had shrunk to the width of the bone while my elbow and forearm were 3 times their normal size. In Addu, the lowest of the Maldives, an atoll with maybe 300 residents in one of the smallest countries in the world, I was able to buy sixty 500mg tablets of Cipro for 10 Dollars. We all like to complain about the drug companies but still we are talking about over a 5000% mark up here charged to people whose taxes help these companies get started. The price of pharmaceuticals continues to soar. The rest of the world gets the medicine for a fraction of the price. We foot the bill.

Karen's Mom never forgave herself for not rotating her eggs on the door of her refrigerator. But who would think of it in normal day to day living? Back at the hospital in Venice, I stared down Nurse Crochet, demanding money, and told the admitting nurse I was leaving and leaving now. We received one bill from the hospital. I sent them a very evil note and they lost heart.

Nevertheless, Americans continue to pay enormous health care costs even though the constitution guarantees us life; along with liberty and the pursuit of happiness. It seems I have strayed from Falcon's education. Sorry, fellow adventurer, sometimes I forget this book is a romantic adventure, not a tirade by yours truly.

In Key West we picked up another delivery. But there was no room on board for Falcon.

"Why should we pay some guy to help you out?" Karen said. "I have turned into one hell of a good sailor, you have said so yourself. Or were you just trying to get laid?" I could see anger sparking dangerously in the back of her eyes. And anyway, she was right. She was a great sailor. But, what were we to do with Falcon?

FSG to the rescue! Michaelanne, who was also anchored in Key West, offered to watch Falcon for us. It was a lot to ask and it was a lot to trust. We had known them for maybe a month. And then, we had only shared dinners, maybe at the most, twice. Should we do it? Karen was torn. She loved adventure but Falcon was her one and only. Anne, the female part of Michaelanne, and Karen spent the day together getting to know one another. In the end Falcon spent a week on Michaelanne and Karen had a bit of adventure.

The delivery was a leaky boat. It was no problem till we rounded the west end of Cuba and headed into the full force of the Caribbean trade winds. The fore hatch didn't close properly and we had a waterfall down below. It took both of us to fix it. One of us stood on the hatch and wiped the hatch with a towel to dry it from the continual spray and the other applied the duct tape. I had bought Karen a new foul weather jacket with the delivery's prepayment, but she didn't want to get it wet. So she went forward naked! On our return, Falcon was very happy to have his mother back and Karen hugged and hugged and hugged Falcon.

In Saint Augustine we rebuilt the stern adding a swim step/sugar scoop/bustle. The boat looked really beautiful with her new stern and a paint job. Naturally the first thing I did on entering the intercoastal was to run aground going around a huge barge. At least everyone passing was able to see our beautiful paint job; bottom and sides both. We wandered up the intercoastal till we arrived at the Chesapeake Bay. We worked our way up the Potomac River. We anchored off the Capitol Yacht Club in Washington D.C. and we bought Falcon a little bike with training wheels that he loved. He had no trouble learning to ride what with his recent success with rowing the dinghy. This was in July and it was hot and humid! Everyday we went to the Smithsonian, four blocks away, which had cold, cold air conditioning. To get there, Falcon rode his little bike on the sidewalk and very conscientiously stopped at every corner to await our arrival with great distain because of our slow pace! When we first started walking to the museum we worried that he would try to cross the street without us. This was D.C. after all and cars zipped by. No worries, Mate. Growing up on a boat was making him into a very responsible young man. Death lurked behind every corner at sea and the desire to risk something for the thrill of it is quickly ironed out.

The Smithsonian was great. Normally we would have rushed through doing it all in a day. Now, everyday for two weeks we explored the museum. There are so many hands-on exhibits that one day explorers just don't have time for.

The reason we went to the Chesapeake in the first place was to visit where Beau Soleil had been built; and learn a bit of her history.

Falcon was starting to develop a love for history. We stopped in Oxford, Maryland and up the Trappe River, where Beau Soleil had been built. Getting a feel for ones roots is important for sailors, because we have so few of them.

Soon summer and its hurricanes was over and we headed south through the Dismal Swamp, which we learned was built by George Washington for his logging business, and headed towards Beaufort.

We had met a young woman in Whidbey Island when we took the train over land to visit with my parents, that summer. She wanted some sea time and we could always use the money. So we offered her a ride. Anyway, twelve hours out to sea, heading towards the Virgin Islands she told us,

"I hope we get into some really nasty weather, maybe a storm. I want to see the ocean at its worse."

Now, the North Atlantic is the last place in the world to say such things. And, Fellow Adventurer, you know what happened next. Karen said at one time the waves were higher than the spreaders. We were hove to for 36 hours till the gale passed over us.

The Virgin Islands were kind to us. We found a great spot for the boat on St. John, I got a job driving a dive boat, and Karen got a job teaching 5th and 6th grades in a private school. Falcon went to a 99% black grade school attending 1st grade. Karen felt bad about not home schooling him from the get go. With both of us working we had no time for him and didn't feel comfortable leaving such a young child on the boat by himself all day long. In retrospect, he would have done fine; maybe. After six months working for her school Karen earned the right to enroll Falcon in her school for free. Falcon did have a few problems acclimating to the public school, but nothing he couldn't handle.

Karen collecting water in Rascal

Educational Experience

First Grade Bravery

On arriving on St. John in the U.S. Virgin Islands, Falcon was ready for first grade. Karen was hired to teach at a private grade school up on the top of a mountain but couldn't get free tuition for her son until she had worked there for at least one semester. We enrolled Falcon at the public school down in the town of Cruz Bay. Other yachties around the anchorage were aghast. They told us how violent the public school was and how dangerous it could be.

"If you're not going to drive him he will have to take the bus. And the school is 99% black!" we were told. Well, we were in the West Indies after all. What did they expect? Falcon at this point had only spent 2 years in the United States, the rest of his life in Central America, Mexico, the Islands and for the first few months, Europe. He was used to non-white faces. And as for violence the first 3 grades were in a different compound, fenced off from the rest of the student body, so any big bullies were kept away.

All went well at first. But after a month I was called to the principal's office at his school. I thought being sent to the principal's office ended with graduation. I didn't know that it started again with parenthood!

It seemed that the 3rd grade had a tree fort that was reserved for 'upper classmen'. Falcon, a true believer of tree forts, had climbed up and made himself at home. A big fight erupted. Three black third graders against one white first grader seemed unfair until you remember that the first grader had been hardened by the sea. The fight erupted into the street; the only road between one side of the island and the other. Traffic was grid-locked for miles in both directions. Eventually the teachers broke it up and I was called in and was asked to please tell my son that he couldn't go into the tree house till he was in third grade and to tell him he had to stop being a bully if he was to stay in school! The whole island was on his side and he was a two week wonder. Never did we have so many dinner invitations. Everyone wanted to meet this little kid hero. He did make some good friends in school, black of course, and after being home schooled for kindergarten he was miles ahead of his class.

He had mixed feelings about moving up the hill to Karen's predominately white grade school after the required 6 months had passed. He did make more friends up there; however, whenever we went to town he wandered off to the playground to have a great time with his old friends.

_/) _/) _/)

Part of his problem adjusting to his new private school was he had to stay at school until his mom was ready to go home. The first thing Falcon did in his new school was to start and organize his fellow second graders to build a fort; and everyone was invited to partake no matter what grade. To help build the fort Falcon brought a table knife to school. This was long before the present trend of school violence but still you should have seen the feathers fly! Part of the problem was I had ended up collecting knifes. Karen never knew what to buy me for my birthday and when asked I replied,

"As long as I have you, Falcon and a boat I am as happy as an anchor in blue mud." I couldn't really ask for something for the boat as it cost so much. As a result Karen usually bought me a knife for birthdays. So Falcon was predisposed to carry a knife. Still he should have asked first.

Between First and Second Grades we sailed down island as far as Antigua. It was a great time wandering aimlessly between islands, exploring, swimming, and loving. We met many boats cruising with children and home schooling. All of the children seemed so well adjusted. Karen, being Karen, just watched, smiled and listened.

Falcon's favorite beach was the windward side of Barbuda. It was a castaway's paradise. Hundreds of glass balls had washed up with the tide and surf. Falcon was determined to collect them all and he and I built a makeshift sled to carry his booty. I tried, to no avail, to convince him that he should collect his goodies on the way back. How he struggled to pull his sled through the soft sand! Finally, after 3 miles, he gave up. He talked me into helping him bury his treasure trove and we returned with one ball and memories to last a life time. In Antigua, we received news that my father had died and we turned north, back to the real world.

We got our share of hurricanes while we were in the Virgins with the occasional 5 to scare us. So when Marilyn a Force 1 at the time, hit St. Croix, 40 odd miles south of us, we didn't become too worried. Within 14 hours Marilyn became a very strong 5 and the eye went over us.

The secret of surviving a 5 is to have a really good hidey hole. If your hole is good enough it becomes an exciting experience rather than a terrifying one. We had been on St. John long enough to qualify to get into the local's 'secret' hurricane hole. Karen and Falcon brought the boat over there for Luis also a 5 that came by a week earlier but gave the Virgins a wide berth. It had hit St. Martin square on and sunk over a thousand boats. I was in San Diego at the time attending my father's funeral. Karen and Falcon drove the boat over to the hole and secured her admirably with three anchors and five lines into the mangroves. Mangroves are the best trees to tie to, as even though they are small, they are immensely strong with huge root systems.

I got back 20 hours before a little Force 1 called Marilyn was due to hit St. Croix and dissipate. Instead it turned north, headed for us and intensified in 40 odd miles into a strong Category 5 hurricane. Marilyn was to be that rarity, a daylight storm. Most evil weather on boats takes place between 3 and 4 o'clock in the morning. No one knows why, it is a mystery. Hurricanes are no different; they love to hit boats when they can hide their fury from human eyes.

Faithful Reader and soon to be thrilled Adventurer, I have a problem. How can I describe such a storm? The first thing you should know is time stops in situations like these. Nothing happens for a long time and then everything happens all at once. Because I could not see everything at once I am going to slip into third person for this description with your permission.

It started about 9 in the morning with a low moaning sound. Beau Soleil was so well protected by surrounding hills that no wind reached her yet. All the crews of the various boats were busy checking their lines. Some crews then left their boats to fend for themselves and headed for houses on land, including the trimaran just to the starboard of Beau. Falcon climbed up to the spreaders and saw the characteristic black arch of an approaching intense tropical low. Soon the wind increased and the wind indicators on top of the masts started to move. In this part of St. John there were six bays all filled with boats. We had eleven in our bay, over 250 all over this part of island. Just in Charlotte Amalie and Water Island, over on St. Thomas, there were over 800 boats. In Beau Soleil's hurricane hole, the rain had started and the wind was up to 30 knots. Not that the crew felt it. The surrounding hills deflected the wind from the bay but wind found its way in with downdrafts. The puffs of wind came straight out of the black low flying clouds and hit the water in the middle of the bay creating a hole and little waves that went on to gently rock the anchored boats.

Ashore, as the wind exceeded 80 knots, coconuts and trash on the ground were catapulted by the wind and became deadly missiles. Most houses had covered their windows with plywood. A few whose owners still believed the forecasters that Marilyn was a Force 1 hurricane and had left their windows unprotected and were forced to evacuated to storm shelters as their homes, the wind having something to worry like a dog, were demolished before their eyes.

As the wind exceeded 150 Knots, a middle hatch on Beau Soleil, left open a eighth of a inch, was violently thrown open and back, in a sudden gust, breaking the half inch bulletproof lexan. Ashore, a family was sitting on a couch in their living room, huddling away from the storm, when their house was torn and lifted from its foundation and thrown down into a valley leaving them, still sitting on a sofa, exposed to the wind and rain but otherwise untouched. In Coral Bay, on the southeastern side of St. John, a lady was so frightened by the increasing conditions on her boat she decided to swim to shore. She had been a championship swimmer in her youth and had no fear of the water. However the wind picked up her body as she tried to dive in and before she hit the water the wind threw her 150 yards into the mangroves where she died instantly; her body crucified by the jagged ends of hundreds of broken off branches.

As the wind approached 200 knots the trimaran next to Beau Soleil became airborne. Mike swam over and filled the amas, the side hulls, with water to keep the unattended boat from flying into the mangroves. Soon boats started to drag. Mike and his friend Jeff swam around retying boats to the trees and to each other. Ashore 95% of the houses had lost their roofs, every telephone pole on the island had been flattened and over 200 boats sunk or destroyed. Over on St. Thomas 450 boats had sunk by this time and the entire island had lost power and water. The eye wall approached St. John. The wall had tornados embedded in it revolving around the eye. The wind exceeded 250 knots, the highest any instrument could measure as the wall hit. The down drafts in Beau Soleil's anchorage were now hitting so hard they drove a hole down into the water all the way to the bottom and created waves the rushed outwards to the shores of the almost circular bay and then ricocheted back into the middle where they smashed into each other creating a huge water spout that was quickly torn away by the wind. By this time Mike and Jeff had created a spider web of lines all over the bay. Afterwards Mike's comment was,

"I just couldn't believe how peaceful it was under the water. And the most amazing thing was thousands of jelly fish had come into our bay and had pushed their heads against the bottom and were swimming down with all their strength. The sand bottom was wall to wall jelly fish."

On the evening of the storm Karen sat huddled from the wind in the cockpit and watched the swiftly changing colors of the violent sunset while tightly hugging her son, kissing him on the head over and over again.

On the western side of St. John, four Hinckleys had been thrown onto the beach and crushed by the huge waves. Afterwards the biggest piece of the fiberglass yachts anyone could find was four feet by two feet. On St. Thomas 790 yachts had sunk. Afterwards, days later, many bodies were found from the sunken boats washed up on small islands and beaches. Ashore, the end of the world had come. The National Park did all right. Of course, it had existed there on St. John for centuries. Everywhere else buildings were demolished, people killed and cars and houses blown away never to be found.

In the middle of the eye all became calm and people came out of whatever defenses they had found only to have the danger multiply a hundred fold. As the wind switched 180 degrees all the sections of sheet metal roofing, coconuts, branches, cars, pets, bicycles, shards of glass and odds and ends all of which had found equilibrium with the previous wind and which piecemeal had become missiles, all instantly became airborne and flew with deadly force against anything still standing. Anyone still outdoors gazing in awe at nature at its most dramatic was instantly killed. Luckily the storm did not stall over the island and pulverize it, but moved on to terrorize other islands.

The next morning wails for the dead filled the now gentle trade winds. People came out and stared at the remnants of their lives. For the next 9 months the island was without power. FEMA came to help, however the disaster was so complete there really was little they could do except supply food and clean water. No grocery stores were left. Banks were shut down for weeks and then only reopened in trailers. The entire island cooked over camping stoves out in the open or under makeshift tents whatever food they could gather. The airport on St. Thomas opened after a week and many left swearing they would never return. The rest fought to remake their lives.

Here I am again. Yes, I still here! Thought you had lost me, did you? No such luck! Our lives didn't change. We sailed over to Tortola in the British Virgins, which was spared, to buy groceries and do laundry. The boat was unscathed save a broken hatch and a broken cleat on the dinghy. We had our own power from solar panels. We were used to catching our own water. Karen normally carried six months of basic food on board so we only had to add fresh provisions to keep going. We still had our music, our movies and when the TV stations came back up we could keep in touch with the busy world still ignoring the Virgins.

With Karen's encouragement her school started back up 3 days after the storm. It gave the children an illusion of normalcy. Her principal and his family lived in the most wretched conditions as did all the staff. It made us feel guilty and blessed at the same time. There were also so many yachties lost, boats sunk, with no where to go except away. The thing was so many had kept their boats in normal anchorages, instead of finding a hole to hide in. Sure, they had jobs to keep which they would lose if they went and hid for every storm that came along. Most were not true yachties but live-a-boarders, camping in style. They were not prepared for Mother Nature on a very bad air day.

All the tourists on the island abandoned ship as did my captain job, so I painted houses to help repair the island and make a few bucks. At first we tried to help out, inviting people out to the boat for dinner and to watch a movie. We had to stop. The despair in their eyes when it was time to leave, to go ashore and return to their makeshift camps, was just too hard for us to take.

Life went on and as winter waned and Falcon completed his second year of school, we decided to return to our sailing lifestyle. Hurricane season threatened again and Karen didn't want to go through it all over yet again. St. John just got power returned to the island and she didn't want to watch it all destroyed again. We couldn't decide to head to Europe or to the South Pacific. We couldn't decide which. To solve our dilemma we asked Falcon.

"Falcon do you want to go visit all the neat castles and museums of Europe and the Med or go see some more beaches in the South Pacific?" He looked at us like we were asking a trick question. "Well, the beaches, of course!"

Off we went down island visiting each island for a few days. In Trinidad we enrolled Falcon in a sailing program. True, he knew a lot about sailing but he had a lot of fun racing and capsizing with the local boys. He made a good friend and went to the movies and had dinner with his family several times during the months we were there. Karen liked the material stores. For some reason Cairo and Port of Spain are the two biggest material cities in the world. They both have store upon store upon store with hundreds of thousands of bolts of material. In Trinidad, easily, 10 city blocks were nothing but cloth stores. Karen, a seamstress from way back, was in seventh heaven. She remade all the upholstery down below and in the cockpit.

Soon we visited Venezuela, the ABC's, the Aves, and Columbia's Cartagena. Cartagena, where we visited in Tola, was much the same. We found a lumber yard where rose wood was selling at give away prices and I built some lockers for the forepeak, Falcon's berth. He had learned enough sailing skills to warrant 'owning' more lockers.

Christmas was coming and we decided to spend it in San Diego with my mother, her first Christmas without my father. The plane tickets to San Diego were very, very expensive. However the tickets to Miami were very cheap. We were toying with the idea of flying to Miami and trying to get some stand by tickets to San Diego, when we found out by accident a little known reality of life.

Because so many cartel members flew into Miami and instead of renting a car, simply stole the first one they saw, the car companies gave anyone flying to Miami from Columbia a free car for a week per adult passenger. Our little greedy eyes lit up and a plan was set. We flew to Miami got our free two weeks, rented the car for two more weeks and drove to San Diego. Not having knife wounds across our faces or wearing Armani suits, the car company wasn't happy about the free weeks and gave us a little Geo Metro, their smallest car. Somehow we managed to squeeze into the car by stopping our laughing for a minute and drove off. Falcon found the back seat folded down and proceeded to make a little camp right in the trunk and back seat areas. The gas tank only held enough fuel for three hours of freeway driving, no doubt to keep cartel members in Miami. For us it was perfect. Every two hours we stopped for fuel and changed drivers. We were used to standing watch on watch.

We stopped at all the sights. What a wonderful trip! Particularly great were the Alamo, Carlsbad Caverns and the Grand Canyon. A week later we pulled into Coronado still laughing. We had a wonderful visit and kept making excuses to prolong our stay until we had to leave and leave now to make our flight in Miami. We drove straight across the country from San Diego to Venice, Florida in 22 hours. I think the cops didn't stop us because they said to themselves, 'my instruments must be off. A Geo Metro can't go that fast!'

After Cartagena we went to the San Blas Islands and fell even deeper in love. These are the islands where the women sew beautiful Molas, reverse appliqué designs inspired by the animals and life around them. As beautiful as the Molas are the islands are even more spectacular. Do you know the classic castaway cartoon island with three coconut trees? That is the San Blas islands. Falcon liked the idea that he could pick a coconut off the ground and bring it to the store where he could buy something worth 25 cents. For four coconuts he could get a soda. The store was 20 miles from where we were but that didn't stop his dreaming. He decided he needed to learn to sail better so he could bring his coconuts to market. In those days everyone sailed. The most popular trade goods for molas were bed sheets the locals turned into sails. We had a wind surfer that he liked because it was much faster than his sailing/rowing dinghy. He wore his harness around his body and I tied the tether to the mast. At first he was swept off the stern of the board by the force of the water but soon he learned to hang on tightly. Within a few weeks he was standing up. Sailing it himself was harder. He was not tall enough to get a good angle to pull the sail, full of water, up off the surface and then to ease off the strain before falling backwards. There is a steep learning curve learning to sail a windsurfer.

In a way all these difficult things he wanted to do were great for his studies. There are few things as difficult as the learning of the Bermuda sling and the windsurfer. In his studies if he didn't understand something instantly, he was used to having to work at learning, to do it. He didn't like it. It was very frustrating. He complained a lot. But he was used to having to work hard to accomplish what he wanted.

The Panama Canal was next; exciting, historic, adventurous and a photo-opportunity. It was all those things, I guess. For a sailor it was down right dangerous now that the Panamanians had taken control of more and more of the canal. Stories abounded about yachts lost in the canal; lost by being crushed by tugs, lost by being thrown against the wall by the ship's wake in front of them, lost by the line handlers above you missing the boat when they threw the monkey fist, lost in the turbulence of the filling lock. And as if that wasn't enough, there was a very real chance sailors would get killed in Colon on the Caribbean side on the canal. It was a very dangerous city. Everyone is warned not to walk around the town. Rape is common place, death is daily. The government doesn't care about your boat. People waste tens of thousands of dollars suing Panama and the canal authority, they just ignore you. They don't care. They have the only game in town.

Actually the government does try. A few years ago the cruise ships threatened to stop calling in at Colon because of the excessive violence. The thugs would line up for blocks around the docks waiting for victims. One day the government announced three ships were coming in at 11 o'clock. At 10:50 three covered trucks pulled up at the dock, dropped their camouflage exposing 50 caliber machine guns and fired at everything that moved. Over three thousand people were killed. The violence eased off for a few weeks but soon was back to full force.

Benny from 'Angelica' had to return to Sweden on business and was going to leave Elizabeth alone on the boat in Colon. Before he left they went together to the local dollar store and Elizabeth bought the cheapest shirt, pants and shoes they had. Now she had the freedom of the city. All the bad guys took one look at her and saw only a dirt poor beggar that could only afford to shop at the cheapest store in town and ignored her, for 6 weeks! Others, not so

135

original, took one step into Colon and lost their money, some teeth, and all their innocence.

We were told at the club that we had to take a taxi everywhere. Irregardless, Karen, Falcon and I would walk to the grocery store and take a taxi filled with groceries, back. When we passed gangs, I let the thin sheath of civilization drop from my eyes and bared the animal beneath. No one bothered us.

Boats transiting the canal are required to be crewed by a captain and 4 line handlers. Rather than pay some locals to be line handlers most owners help each other out crewing on their friend's boat then, their friends, on theirs. It is good fun plus it gives the novice a first hand look at the operation before it is his turn to put his boat at risk. We had no problems. Because we had been through before on Beau and because the price goes down each time you go through we only had to pay $38. Part of the reason is we got a beginner pilot. It was his first transit in charge and I spent half the time telling him what to do next!

Falcon was great. He did his job and jumped around fixing things before they became an issue. Of course, he had been a line handler before when he was 1½. Karen as always was perfection and beauty in motion. It must be the teacher in her. She saw everything. The smallest item out of place couldn't escape her tidying swan like hands. Me? I drove the boat, kept the pilot in check, and made sure the beer was cold for the celebration assuming we would escape and make it through unscathed yet again.

The problem is I didn't have command over the whole operation. No one else did either. True, it was such a well oiled machine, little went wrong. But when it did, what a mess! However once again we made it through despite one line thrower who was the slowest man in the world. He threw his line 5 times before we caught it and each time he spent 3 minutes pulling in his 100 foot line. With judicious backing and filling we managed to maintain our place in the canal despite the doors closing and water starting to fill the lock in torrents.

The Pacific was great. So quiet compared to the windy Caribbean. We had a wonderful celebration at the Balboa Yacht Club, having somehow beaten fate yet once again.

Falcon learning to Windsurf

A FLEET OF CHILDREN

They call it the milk run. Like it is supposed to be so easy. Wander gently through the South Pacific visiting beautiful paradises and end up in New Zealand or Australia or Fiji for the hurricane season. Never get winds above 20 knots. It sounded so great. It sounded so wonderful. Too bad it wasn't true.

The milk run starts in Galapagos, no, really Panama. In Panama we seriously stocked up. All the way across the Pacific we would not be able to buy stores for a reasonable price, until we arrived in Fiji. This was important for those of us that were still trying to keep employment to a bare minimum. This was especially true in French Polynesia where the prices were absurd, we were told. Karen packed food into the boat with a shoe horn. There was food everywhere; our waterline went up 7 inches (or the boat went down 7 inches depending on the level of rum in your glass.) Falcon was really a great help, he took it seriously, like kids sometimes do. That's not fair. He took anything to do with food seriously! He was in charge of labeling everything and keeping inventory. He had papers everywhere full of notes. His education was definitely starting to pay dividends. With Karen's help he organized his notes into a proper report with charts and flow diagrams, no less! All colored in exciting vibrant colors, but you already knew that was going to happen, right? We had found some triangular shaped crayons in Cartagena that fit young hands perfectly. Why don't they have such great things in the States?

When we went to San Diego for Christmas, we picked up volumes of third grade school work. We had looked into Calvert and Oak Meadows home schooling systems. It seemed to cost a lot for what we would receive. Perhaps if we could turn in the work and receive it back quickly it would be better. (These days it would be via e-mail, back then it was snail mail.) We moved around so much it was difficult enough for our regular mail to catch up with us, much less something sent bulk rate. For 5% of what we would have paid, we set Falcon up for school. We had work for math, science, English, French and Spanish, geography, history, and penmanship. He wasn't very enthusiastic about the school work but he was against a united front, dug in and entrenched. We were insistent about the foreign languages. Karen spoke beautiful French and I, horizontal Spanish, learned years ago, before I met Karen. Horizontal languages are learned flat on your back and have a somewhat limited vocabulary. It is a great way to learn a language as there are certain times when a man is very open to new ideas, new thoughts and words!

In the Virgins we had become Ham Radio Operators and in the Caribbean we had used the single-side band radio for receiving weather reports. Now we found we were a part of a huge armada crossing the Pacific that kept in touch every day on the radio! Every morning we 'met' at established times for the radio net. We talked about how the night at sea went, what the weather might be doing, and contacted boats in front of us for info on roadblocks in clearing customs in the next port. For the women, especially, it was a high point of a day at sea. At times it sounded like a sewing bee there was so much gossip. It didn't take long for the kids to set up their own net. They spent most of their time on air encouraging each other to get months worth of school work finished at sea so they could play on the beach all day long when they arrived in the Marquesas.

The passage from the Las Perlas Islands, just off Panama, to the Galapagos took a lazy ten days. Not much wind, but then we weren't expecting much, if any. We cleared in at San Cristobal; not voluntarily. We arrived on Easter Sunday so we felt the customs officials, in a very catholic country, would be occupied in church, so we gave ourselves the freedom of the port rather than wait till Monday. Unfortunately at 10 AM we were boarded (yes, Dear Reader, again) our passports seized and we were told to report first thing tomorrow morning along with five other boats equally caught.

It was worth the trouble. We had a great time. Falcon rode up and down the streets on the back of a 150 year old giant tortoise. We had to pick our landing beaches with care lest on our return, our dinghy was occupied by several very large sea lions! Penguins kept swimming around the boat, which I loved. A long time ago, in a different life it seems, I was the second person ever to breed an Adelie penguin in captivity. These are the ones who live in Antarctica. Falcon learned more about penguins during that week than he ever really wanted to know. We spent a lovely two weeks on San Cristobal and Santa Cruz. Santa Cruz had the Charles Darwin Research Center, where Falcon spent many a happy hour. How many school kids get to have a field trip to the Galapagos?

We made it to the Marquesas in 24 days. Some times we had the spinnaker up for three days in a row, day and night, as the wind was so light. Once, when Karen was on watch, she missed seeing a squall sneak up behind her. By the time I rushed on deck it was blowing 35 knots and we were going so fast the bow wave towered above the deck. The spinnaker sheets were solid, man, rock solid. Karen's knuckles were as white as death as she steered the boat and surfed down the waves. She knew that one mistake and we would lose the mast. What a brave little girl, when I asked her if she wanted me to take over, she said,

"I got us into this mess; I'll get us out of it." All this through clenched teeth! Little did we know that these squalls would be great practice for later, when we were down where hell really breaks loose, in the Southern Ocean's roaring forties.

We stopped at Fatu Hiva first. This is not really a clearance port but it is the first island we came to and the most spectacular and it was on the way, kind of. As we came into the bay, six huge black basalt spurs, 300 feet high, looking ever so much like pagan Tiki gods, loomed over us in haughty splendor. They came in pairs, one of each on either side of the entrance. We had to pass between each pair in turn. I almost felt like cowering beneath their fierce glares. Me! At the base of the bay, a black sand beach lay with a few black rocks lurking just awash. Above the black on black of the beach, green coconut palms feathered the valley. Above the palms, in the distance, the white of a waterfall broke the black mountains into two halves. Below the palms, the colorfully dressed Marquesans played soccer, darting this way and that like so many birds. Not many first impressions are as fabulous as this. No wonder so many of Bligh's men mutinied!

Because there were no banks on the island and the locals had no need of foreign currency, or any currency for that matter, they were used to bartering. The men playing soccer took one look at the brace on my knee and were willing to trade anything, well almost, for it.

Back in Venezuela when I was playing football with Falcon on a beautiful white sand beach with nice hard packed sand, I hurt my knee. Chasing down the ball, I ran at full speed from hard pack into deep soft sand. My foot and leg sunk down into the sand up to my knee; my body kept going. The pain was indescribable. Ten days later we arrived in the civilization of Puerto La Cruz and Karen got a doctor to come out to the boat. He took one look and turned white. His eyes looked so sad. He then gave me the best advice ever.

"You have to walk on it, no matter how much it hurts, or you will loose the leg. Everyday, walk as far as you can."

It took five years. Five years of living hell, but today, my leg is stronger than it ever was. Part of my self imposed rehabilitation was wearing a knee brace. This was the brace the Marquesans wanted. The good ones have a little hole in the middle where the knee cap is.

Karen traded more kid clothes (what else?) and perfume for fresh veggies and fruit. She asked why the women wanted perfume when they were surrounded by the indescribable heavenly aroma of the South Seas.

"Our husbands are tired of the smell of flowers. They want something different," she was informed. Falcon traded American marbles for French marbles that looked totally the same but, I was told emphatically, were very valuable. And neither had come from China he informed me with a steely look!

Slowly, the kid boats started to dribble in. Finally, he could put faces to the names and personalities he had come to know on the radio during the last 3 weeks. As a group we wandered thru the islands to Anaho Bay where even more kid boats had ended up.

Malcolm, 10, and Naomi 8 were on 'Gumboot'. Eileen, 12 and Greg, 6, on 'Jump Up', were some of Falcon's favorites. Just as adults on cruising boats quickly made friends so did their children. As a group, the crews of 5 or 6 kid boats walked over the island to a bodysurfing beach on the windward side. That helped to break the ice for the kids. They became great friends on that trip and during the next 7 months, as we all sailed the South Pacific together. They have continued their friendships thru e-mail to this day, a decade later.

Soon, we left for an easy passage down to the Tuamotus.   We sailed to Raroia, the atoll where Thor Heyerdahl landed on Kon Tiki. The village lay on a motu close to the entrance where they no longer collect copra. They now breed black pearls.   While the far off motus, or little islands on the surrounding reef, were still owned by various locals, they didn't mind us anchoring off them for as long as we wished.   French Polynesia, of which the Marquesas and Tuamotus were part, restrict visitors to 2 weeks without a cash bond, the equivalent of a plane ticket to your home country each, or 3 months if you paid the bond, payable only in Tahiti. The visiting boat was required to be in Tahiti within 2 weeks of entering the territory. Two weeks to visit the hundreds of islands in the Marquesas and Tuamotus and to sail the 750 miles to Tahiti at an average of 120 miles a day. Not a chance of that happening!   The result is that every boat had already broken the law by the time they arrived in Tahiti.   Most paid the fine gladly having seen a part of the world few ever have the chance to visit. I thought it was a fixed game.

Initially, we were only going to stay in the French Territory a few weeks as who wanted to put up with the French? Little did I know how fantastic the place was. We had such a great time. Even the part about not being able to buy anything in the grocery stores wasn't true. French bread, New Zealand butter and liver (Don't ask, I have no idea why!) were all about the same price as in Hawaii. In the outer islands, the locals told us which mountain to climb to find wild fruit. Every island had its own charm and all of them were charming. We wanted to stay longer. But I didn't want to condone their little money scheme. So I decided not to pay the bond. The Authorities? We would have to keep out of their way. And besides, every paradise has its own form of snake lurking in the grass.

A little hurricane, I stupidly managed to put us in the way of between the Tuamotus and Tahiti, gave us such a pasting it tore half of the name 'Beau Soleil' off of the stern. I sanded the rest off to prepare it for Karen to paint it back on. Just as she was readying her paints I had a grand idea. If we were going to be a mystery boat avoiding the authorities, why should we have an ID? So we officially became the boat with no name!

On Raroia, Falcon, Malcolm and Naomi went native. They did their school work in record time often getting up at 7 in the morning, a rare miracle, then borrowed our rowing dinghy and spent the rest of the day ashore. They caught their own fish and cooked them on sticks held over a fire. They built forts only to be abandoned in a move to a new motu. They climbed coconut trees and ate uu burgers. (Uus are the inside of the coconut after the meat has changed from coconut to a dense fiber out of which the sprout is born. Fried up it tastes vaguely like hamburgers.) They ate the living sprouts born out of fallen coconuts. With our help they ate millionaire's salad, the heart of the coconut tree. Even though it cost a young tree's life to gather the salad, there were so many trees, most died for lack of sunshine and space. The fallen coconuts covered the island's sand beaches. Normally these would be picked up for copra, now the locals had more lucrative ventures.

The three children got along together unbelievably well. Never was a cross word, or an ego's voice, heard. In a way it was unfortunate for Falcon. In the future all of his friendships would be measured by these ones, born in a time of imagination gone wild. Later, when a grown up's expediency replaced the child's imagination, the power of these friendships would still remain as a burning eternal flame in the altar of memory, condemning almost all future relationships to second rate status at best.

The spear fishing was great. Finally, I had reached the point on the learning curve where I easily could kill enough to feed my family. I speared with Robert on 'Deusa', originally from Zimbabwe, a big game hunter of some repute. He complemented me on the excellence of my ability to shoot straight into the brain, killing instantly. Robert gave Falcon a Bermuda sling of his own. Now he could fish with his old man. Karen, Falcon and I almost always speared together. The snake in the Eden of Raroia was the number of sharks in the lagoon. Most of them were blacktips. While reaching 10 to 12 feet in length these were fairly placid sharks. As long as one of us kept our eyes on them they would keep their distance. If we all turned our backs, emboldened, they would become aggressive and circle closer and closer working up the nerve for a bite.

Karen was the eyes in our pack. She had a little Hawaiian sling that gave her courage even though it would be worthless in a confrontation. She would poke menacingly at the sharks, growling in her throat and snorkel. Sharks are very sensitive to sound and pick up emotion easily. The growling put the sharks on alert to Karen's anger at them for coming so close. Often, we swam with 5 to 10 sharks, a dangerous habit, but we told ourselves that they were only blacktips. About one in ten would be a whitetip. These were more aggressive sharks. A little smaller, averaging about 9 to 10 feet, they made up for the lack of size with nerve and a bad, nasty attitude. Then to make matters worse, there were the Silkies. Silkies were just plain mean. Bad tempered and about the size of a blacktip, they are dangerous sharks. We always kept two pairs of eyes on the circling pack when Silkies were in the area. They ran in packs, like wolves, and with the same intelligence. Most of the time, the other sharks left the area when Silkies moved in. The worse part was when I caught a lobster. Sharks love lobster and will take your hand right off in the attempt to grab one. We always held them out of the water as we swam them back to the dinghy, out of sight, smell and hearing.

The sharks seemed to recognize me as some kind of alpha male. My inbred aggressiveness matched theirs but as far as I was concerned my little stainless arrow was nothing compared to their teeth. I was running a bluff. Once, Karen and Falcon went spearing by themselves. They were gone only 5 minutes. Without me in the water, they were chased out in no time, by blacktips. There, I knew aggressiveness had some purpose!

The Tigers and Hammerheads mostly stayed out in deeper water, so we didn't see much of them. The Great Whites were a nightmare that, hopefully, stayed far, far away.

Falcon, Malcolm and Naomi would occasionally play with a shark by themselves. It made me very nervous. I told myself that Falcon knew what he was doing. Maybe, if I said that to myself often enough, I would start to believe it. As for Karen, she struggled with indecision. On one hand, she wanted to let her son grow up, but on the other she wanted to protect him at all times. Eventually, she just made sure that they played in very shallow water where all sharks are on the defensive. Sharks are amazing creatures with incredible speed and with the reactions of a kung fu master. Mostly the three children just probed the shark and then just sat back and watched in awe. We never speared or ate shark. It is a Polynesian belief that, if you have eaten shark, other sharks with their incredible sense of smell, can smell it in your skin oils and will attack, instantly and mindlessly. I don't know if I believe it or not, but there are so many other fish, why take chances?

For an outing, we visited the village at the entrance of the lagoon. We checked in with the police station as a courtesy, we were using their lagoon after all; the one policeman for the whole lagoon was off on another motu.

In talking to his wife, the conversation came around to black pearls. She pulled out her personal film canister and emptied out a dozen beautiful pearls. One big one was unusual. It had ring of striations around its equator, looking ever so much like Saturn. After a month in French Polynesia, we still hadn't found a bank, so we asked her if she would like to trade, as we had no Pacific Francs. We racked our brains for something that would be of value on an atoll with no electricity. No, that's wrong. They did have one solar panel to run the TV to watch soccer in the village square. They had all the food they could eat, they built their own houses, and the motus were so small even a bicycle was superfluous. They were rich from their black pearls and could buy what they wanted from Tahiti. We let our minds scan all the different lockers in our boat and what they held that we didn't need ourselves, being as how we were in the back of beyond.

"I got it," Karen whispered, "the typewriter." It was a good idea. We recently had joined the computer age, as much of Falcon's school work was on software. With the word processing applications on the computer and with our printer, we really didn't need my trusty old typewriter any more. I smiled at the chief of police's wife and queried,

"Does your husband have a typewriter for important police matters? Surely Tahiti expects typewritten reports." Her eyes gleamed. It seems her husband's birthday was approaching and she needed a present. We went out to the boat and returned with the typewriter and just like that we were the proud possessors of our very own black pearl.

A week later while cleaning out a drawer, Karen found a new typewriter ribbon we had forgotten about. Within a couple of days, we returned to the village. We visited the police station and there, on a pedestal in the middle of the room, was our old typewriter, illuminated by sunlight reflected by a mirror in the window. When we gave the wife the ribbon, she was so excited she gave us a double pearl carved in the shape of a heart. I guess her husband really liked his present!

Disaster. Just when everything was going so good, the shit hit the fan. 'Gumboot,' Malcolm and Naomi's boat, dragged one night and ended up on the reef. A westerly wind had come up during the night in the Easterly trades region and blown them ashore. They were hard aground lying on their port side. We started work at first light. There isn't much tide in the Tuamotus but what there was, was going to peak that night. It was get her off tonight or write her off as a total wreck.

A German friend was anchored in the same lagoon and the three crews worked together over 12 hours trying to get Gumboot off. At one point Jenny and Bob gave up and asked if I would take them to Tahiti.

"Yeah, I'll take you, if ya really want. But I think we should get your boat off this here reef first. I think it is way too early to give up." We had a 70 lb fisherman anchor which we carried on deck just for hurricanes and situations like this. We used all of Gumboot's winches to pull against that massive anchor. I put Beau off to one side a ¼ mile away and pulled Gumboot sideways from the top of her mast with every line we had tied together. The tide was higher now and the boat more up right but the keel was still stuck on the reef. By pulling sideways from the top of Gumboot's mast, we could lift the keel off the bottom pivoting the boat on its floating hull.

Our German friend pulled straight ahead with his engine. Gumboot wouldn't budge. Again and again we tried. She was a racing boat with a deep, deep keel that was stuck in the sand and coral. Finally, I put an anchor out to one side of Gumboot, sent the anchor line from the anchor thru a block on her mast then back to Beau, out in deep water. I first tried this technique while capturing a baby grey whale for a park and a research institute in San Diego. At first we tried lassoing the whale from a P-Cat (kind of like a Hobie Cat, only different and bigger) but the mother saw us coming and sunk us with a casual swing of her tail. Next we grabbed the baby's tail from the pulpit of a sword fishing boat. As we tried to winch the baby back to the boat the mother started hitting the baby for not obeying her and not getting away from that bad boat. She hit her so hard the baby flew out of the water; all this while the poor 20 foot baby was towing our 70' ship at 4 knots. So quickly we planted an anchor on a sand bar, led the line thru the anchor and out to the ship. The ship motored full ahead and pulled the baby back, stranding her on the sand bar, but away from her mother. The mother and baby cried to each other for hours.

Lest you think badly of me and San Diego, this was for scientific purposes. Killer whales heal perfectly. They never scar. They grow back severed limbs. Dolphins, a close relative, scar badly and never grow back limbs. Grey whales don't scar at all but don't grow back limbs. It was hoped that by studying the grey whale, a related species to both dolphin and killer whale, they could figure which genes were turned on in the killer whale to keep them in perfect trim. A year later the baby, much bigger, was eating $2000 worth of food a day and she was released. I never heard of any miracle gene cures so I guess our efforts were for naught.

Sorry about the journey down memory lane there. This was the trick we tried on Gumboot. We pulled on the line that went from the anchor to the block on the mast and out to Beau with all we had, Jenny and Bob winched like demons and the German boat pulled like gang busters. Slowly she moved and then with a rush she was off. She was free! What a party we had!

Tahiti was a disappointment. The friendliness and peace and quiet of the outer islands was gone and in its place was 'Waikiki meets Paris'. In a few days, we were off to Moorea. What a sea change! All our friends had felt the same. Now, instead of shopping at chic boutiques and eating at French restaurants, we climbed mountains and visited archeological sites. It was good for my bad knee as I stumbled along behind everyone. By the time we reached Bora Bora, we had gone native. We were living the life of beachcombers, but in the comfort of our yachts. Back in States, we had sail boats. In America, we had holes in the water that we poured money, often endlessly, into. Here at the far edge of civilization, we had yachts and lived like kings!

Benny and Elizabeth aboard 'Angelica' had no children with them. In fact, their son back home in Sweden had divorced them, a practice allowed in that country. Nevertheless, children or not, they became part of the kid fleet mostly because of their joie de vivre and fun loving customs. In Sweden, after the harvest in fall, all the people in the cities, partake in the rite of palla and go out into the fields and collect the left over fruit and vegetables from the fields. With us, it started fairly sanely. The French were building a new road right thru a garden and were throwing all the dirt, rocks and veggies that were in the way, over to the side of the road. What a waste. It was too much for the Swedes. This was a case for palla-man if there ever was! Benny and Elizabeth pulled along side Beau, jumping up and down in their dinghy in excitement and forced us to go palla-ing with them. Who said Polynesia was expensive? After filling our lockers with veggies, we hiked far up into the mountains to collect wild bananas, guavas and mountain apples. This might seem tame to you, Dear Reader, but remember we were a bunch of sailors with the most rudimentary knowledge possible of the vegetable kingdom. The way we acted made it seem a mosquito bite was as bad as a tiger attack! It is amazing we didn't poison ourselves, by giving each other things to eat,

"Benny, eat this. I think it smells really good." But we came down off that mountain like great white hunters returning with a kill, our bags full with food. The governor of Tahiti had a palace on Huahine with gardens planted with lime trees. One afternoon after an alcoholic tea party, we decided it was time for palla. We snuck up on the trees like army men, crawling on our hand and knees. We loaded up our little bags and snuck back out giggling the whole time. Once, I looked over at the Polynesian guards by the gate. They were laughing up their sleeves! Damn, but we had a good time in French Polynesia!

Time was marching on, and we had a long way to go before the hurricane season started, so it was with heavy hearts that we said goodbye to French Polynesia and headed towards Tonga and trouble.

The Pacific always has a lot of hurricanes. We don't hear much about them as they don't threaten American interests. This was not the hurricane season yet, but we had already been through one hurricane at sea between the Tuamotus and Tahiti a month before. Now we were going to go thru another. The storm was 24 hours away. Luckily, a little island called Nuie was close by. The only anchorage it had was wide open to the increasing wind and seas but the island was nearly circular in shape with high cliffs along the sea. Within a day, we and ten other boats were sailing slowly back and forth under Nuie's lee while the hurricane screamed above us. We had a triple reefed mizzen and a storm jib up not because it was blowing so hard, here, under the lee it was 20 to 25 knots, but because if we went too fast we would sail out of the lee all that much faster and would have to come about more often. Usually at sea in storms like these we were all by our lonesome. Now it was fun to wave to each other as our boats passed. The kid net was going full throttle, mostly about how they were going to tie themselves to giant kites and soar up into the hurricane strength winds far above us. Karen's only comment was to ask for the length of the hypotenuse of the triangle that would be the string. That kept them going for another 30 minutes as they asked their parents in the middle of a hurricane for help with what a hypotenuse was, and how to calculate it.

'Jump Up' got tired of waiting for the hurricane to dissipate. They were a 57' steel ketch and felt that a little category 1 hurricane shouldn't slow down their cruising plans. They left the lee of Nuie bound towards Tonga and good protection. John and Karen thought they could avoid the worse of the storm. Of course, they ended up having to sail right thru the eye. They were terrified! Or at least Karen was.

"I would have had a nervous breakdown if it wasn't for the kids." During the worse of it, they were in the forepeak being thrown around, and playing trampoline on the berths. They kept yelling, 'Do that big wave again, Dad!' The kids were so happy; it was difficult for the adults to be scared.

Nuie was great after the wind stopped. Falcon insisted we rent bikes and tour the island. There were limestone caves and grottos everywhere on the island and good roads to travel between them. Like everywhere else we traveled, Falcon ended up having to write a report on his experience. I called it a field trip which earned me scornful looks from Karen.

"Mike, really, it is part of his lesson plan!"

Karen and I were still on our honeymoon after all these years, yet I could foresee troubled waters lying ahead. She was putting way too much of her time into Falcon's education and not as much on me! Or was I just jealous? Or was I lagging in my efforts on the education instruction situation? I promised to myself to try to take over more of the effort and see if that cleared the muddy waters.

Tonga is the next gathering of the fleet after Tahiti. It is a glorious country and rates along with the San Blas as

the only islands never to be conquered by anyone, at least for the last 3000 years. The original people still live there, before them there was no one. We all
anchored at in front of a likely looking watering hole, which turned out to be kid friendly. They organized a dinghy sailing race for the kids and supplied the prize. As you can imagine this started great interest in sailing dinghies. It seemed that of the 8 kid boats in port, everyone either had a sailing dinghy or could borrow one. The prize was a huge bowl of ice cream. Falcon eventually won the race, only because he listened better to the race instructions. After that, dinghy races were a common occurrence whenever we stopped.

The names of the islands in Tonga are very long and difficult to pronounce. To help with this problem, a charter company years ago put out a map with the 30 or so perfect anchorages labeled with numbers. Now, if you made a date to meet up with another boat, instead of saying 'lets anchor together at Malafakalava', you could say 'let's meet at #6.' Years ago when I came here on Time Out the numbers were just getting started and were viewed with scorn by the locals. When we passed thru on Beau, even the locals were starting to refer to different spots by their number name when talking to sailors.

On Karen's birthday, I arranged that we would sailed over to number 11, where a local family was going to put together a Tongan feast in celebration of her birthday. The mother and older girls did the cooking, the older boys served the food for the women and a true beauty served us men. The youngsters did the dancing. It was a great feast. Everything was biodegradable and this was long before it was popular to be ecologically conscious. The table was covered in palm fronds and food served on Ti leafs. Of course, we ate with our fingers. This was the South Pacific, after all. We had lobster, shrimp, pork, many different but delicious vegetables and coconut pudding for dessert that we ate with a carved piece of coconut husk. After dinner, the older family members including one lass whom we nicknamed Minerva, mostly because we couldn't pronounce her real name and she seemed to do her act and then disappear like Minerva Reef, put on a show. I tried to dance and we even got Karen up on the table to do the Tamari. Cost? 10 dollars a head. Many of our cruising buddies showed up to congratulate Karen. We all brought enhancement to add to our coconut water served in the nut and soon the party developed into a no-holds-bared cruising party. That's one party Karen never forgot.

Behind Nuie in a Hurricane

Educational Experience

Falcon Takes Command

In Tonga when Falcon was 10 he took his Mother sailing and discovered that he was better at it than she was. Finally he was good at something! It was her birthday and I had organized to take her to a feast and all our cruising friends were going to show up. We were anchored 5 miles away from the party as the seagull flies. However, extensive reefs made the true distance closer to 15 miles. To get to #11 from #30, where we were anchored that day, required we sail 10 miles out of our way instead of directly across the reef as it was too shallow for Beau, but not for Falcon's sailing dinghy. Falcon insisted that he was going to sail Karen across the reef for an adventure and a birthday present. Karen was very nervous about the whole thing. She kept coming up with reasons why she couldn't go, but he insisted. Such preparation! There is little doubt who Falcon's mother is, they both love to pack. If they had their way, the dinghy would have sunk 5 feet away from Beau. I finally drew the line when I found them installing the GPS and batteries in the little sailing boat. They could see their destination 5 miles away, after all! Finally they were off. Because Karen pretended she was a little apprehensive, Falcon threw in lots of extra gybes going around coral heads. Karen told Falcon that they were being swept out to sea.

"Mom, just relax. We are doing just fine. Now, listen, WATCH OUT FOR THAT BIG OCTOPUS! Ha! Made you look." They were laughing and laughing.

I monitored their progress thru binoculars as I brought Beau around the reefs instead of over them. It was going to be close as to who arrived first. I worked out the variables in my mind. Which would be better for Falcon; to beat his old man or to have to yet again acknowledge his Dad's mastery? If I let him beat me, a little of my authority would be eroded; but, hey, I had plenty left. If I beat him it would reaffirm his underling status.

In the end I threw in a couple of unnecessary tacks and Falcon beat me by 10 seconds. He lorded it over me that night. I let him get away with it. My son had taken a big step towards becoming a man.

_/) _/) _/)

The breeding and calving humpback whales had stopped in the islands and we went out to see them. The deal was, you couldn't race up to see them, but instead approached within a few hundred feet and let them come to you. Well! This was a contest if there ever was one! Who could attract the most whales? We went with 6 other boats and we all spread out where the whales were and did our best to attract them. Falcon's idea was to sing to them. It is a miracle that any showed up at all as my poor son inherited my tone deafness. Karen put classical music on the stereo and I from long years of experience, just waited. Eventually, we had a mom and her calf visit us for 20 minutes, surfacing 10 feet from the drifting boat, till they were chased away by a big bull. I guess he wanted them all for himself. Greedy!

But soon, once again, the far horizons beckoned. Some boats went south to New Zealand, some to Samoa, and some like us to Fiji. We had to wend our way thru myriads of islands and reefs to get to Suva to clear in. Normally we would have been tempted to stop and look around but we had spent so much time in French Polynesia that we only had a few weeks left till hurricane season started. We left for New Zealand from the west side of Fiji where I used to do illegal charters with Time Out. Luckily no one recognized me in a new boat and with a family!

We waited in vain for a good window to sail down to New Zealand. The lows came marching across the Southern Ocean, like clockwork. Even for a fast racer, it took 7 or 8 days to get south and the lows were 5 days apart. No matter what we did we would have to go through some bad weather. Our trip started out fine. Nice sailing, following wind and seas. Now, if it could only stay like this.

Dear Reader and Fellow Adventurer, I hope you have gained enough understanding about our capricious seven seas by now. I know I don't have to tell you we ended up in an evil storm because you already anticipated it. So I won't tell you about it. What? You want the details? You want me to relive that storm? Have you no mercy? Do you like to see me suffer? Do you want my head to explode? Alright, all right. It started out nice. It ended nice. Bad stuff happened in the middle. Will that do? No, I guess not.

Two days out, it started getting rough. It was too late to turn around. Besides, we told ourselves, we've been through rough weather before. We're seasoned sea dogs. That's what I said, I did. Silly me. You would think that by this time I would have known better. So, we battened down the hatches and arranged drip cloths in likely spots where water might squirt in. Within 12 hours it was blowing 45 knots, a lot of wind, and the seas coming up from the Southern Ocean were awesome, to put it mildly. We were now beating into it, and taking a bashing with spray flying all the way to the stern, when the bob stay broke.

We haven't talked about rigging yet. The rigging holds up the masts, which hold up the sails, which hold up our spirits, which – never mind. The bobstay is one of the most important stays and the only one half under water at sea. It goes from the end of the bowsprit to a massive piece of stainless steel sticking out of the boat at the waterline. To fix it, we hove to and Karen and Falcon held my feet as I lowered myself head first, over the 6 foot bow in 30 foot seas. Half the time I was underwater, but Karen and Falcon were getting drenched, too! Eventually, I replaced the broken turnbuckle and tightened it, and retuned the rest of the rig, which had been flopping around, trying to yank the masts out of the boat. All was hunky dory till the next day, when the damn thing broke again! Again it was the turnbuckle. I guess I should have known when I bought them for $5 a piece at a flea market that it was a deal too good to be true. We went thru the whole bit again. This time, I was a bit faster, being as how, I was practiced up and all.

When we talked about the first breakage on the daily radio net, we received dozens of calls of well wishers and lots of 'well done's' when we fixed her. When we related our second disaster, we received dead silence. I could just hear what people were thinking, during the prolonged silence. 'What kind of boat is that anyway?' 'Can't they fix any thing right?' 'And we were supposed to be their friends?'

After the gods had taught me yet again to be humble, and to be sure to check everything 3 times before going to sea, they let us go and we had a easy sail into the Bay of Islands.

Who Wouldn't Sail with This Lady

CROSSING THE TASMAN

They wanted to pirate all our fresh produce when we entered the Bay of Islands. We knew it was going to happen from the horror stories on the Ham radio told by the boats in front of us and we tried our best to eat everything on board, but even with our big eater, Falcon, we failed. We had a dozen Fijian eggs and a big pumpkin and a few onions left. As Karen started to hand over her carefully selected veggies and eggs with tears in her eyes, her natural rapport with people came to our rescue. That and Falcon was doing his best to look famished. That was difficult to do. Do you remember the old Charles Atlas ads that had the 99 pound weakling, and then the picture six months after? Falcon already looked like the 'after' at nine. It wasn't his fault. He lived in a very demanding and athletic lifestyle. Anyway the poor officials didn't know what hit them. They finally said,

"All we really want is the shells of the eggs and the rind of the pumpkin. If you quickly cook the rest you can keep them. The rinds and the shells carry the infestations."

Did I ever tell you Karen makes the best pumpkin pie? Yeah, Mon! She made three of them. We tried to get our Quarantine Official to take home a pie, but he wouldn't hear of it. Already, I was starting to like New Zealand. Honest officials? What a refreshing change!

The Bay of Islands has to rank right up there with Fatu Hiva, as one of the great approaches in the world. As your boat enters the bay, a myriad of islands appear. Each is covered with the greenest grass ever, a spattering of trees and thousands of sheep which roam their steep slopes. But, there are so many islands; the sheep seem to be just dotted here and there and their rain washed white wool emphasizing the greenness of their surroundings. Delving deeper in between the islands brings you to Opua, the clearance port in these parts. There isn't much to it, but then what do sailors need besides a grocery store, a post office, a laundromat and a bar. How simple is the life of a sailor. Of course, one has to be simple-minded to go to sea in the first place!

The place is quiet; quiet, except for the calls of birds and the murmuring of the sheep. After a wild sail to get here a bit of peace and quiet is just what was needed. Finally, time to relax without worrying about the hurricane season. We were out of range. We were safe! It was so rough coming down that I let Falcon slide on his schoolwork. I expected him to catch up now. Silly me. Didn't I see a new country to explore? New beaches to play on? Falcon was showing every sign of a strike against school work again so we enrolled him in the state run, home school system before the strike reached the stop work stage. He received his New Zealand work by mail and sent it back by same. The state paid for the mailing. It was an interesting course, very strong in math which fortunately, or unfortunately, Falcon needed help in. It lacked a bit in writing and geography. I thought he didn't need the second as he was daily immersed in it, and I felt I could help in the first. They didn't send books but just printouts of the required material. To save postage, I guess. Naturally, he resented the whole affair. He was used to conning his mother to get out of school early, now he couldn't. Like all kids, like all humans, he resented a faceless entity telling him what to do, so we took him to meet his teachers in Wellington, on our camping trip around the North Island.

It was a great trip. We bought a used car for 500 New Zealand dollars and filled it with camping gear and groceries. We couldn't believe how big and light and cheap, tents had become. Soon, we were off. While driving down 90 Mile Beach, Falcon had his first driving lesson. I thought about it first before I let him take the wheel. There weren't any other cars. The beach was totally flat with hard pack sand. The only way he could get into trouble was to drive into the Tasman Sea on the right or bog down on a sand dune to the left. So I gave him the wheel.

When I was 16 my older sister received her first driver's license. The first time she got into the car, she took off at 50 miles per hour down a skinny little alleyway. Falcon was almost as bad. Somehow, I assumed that he would be driving straight down the beach, but no, he drove down in circles. I'm very glad that, one, no one could see us, and two, he was too short to reach the pedals so I was in control of those. Now a days, walking down a beach, I see big tire tracks looping in circles on the beach. I know all about how they were formed! He didn't improve his driving performance after a half-hour so I took back the wheel. In the rear view mirror I could see Karen's hair had just turned white. Just kidding, Karen! Made you look!

The only problem of driving up and down our driving course was getting on and off the beach. There were very few places a normal car could traverse without getting bogged down in soft sand. But we didn't mind. At night, we just stopped and camped. During the day, we climbed sand dunes and slid down them on a piece of cardboard at dizzying speeds or none at all. For some reason, only some dunes had slippery sand, the others, even little Falcon just sat there poised on the top of a very steep sand dune and sat, and sat. I looked at him up there, jumping up and down on his piece of cardboard, trying to make it go and I was reminded of a writing exercise he did the previous week. We had gone for a walk with the intention of climbing a hill that looked interesting from a distance, but on arrival had almost vertical sides for the first 100 feet. I lost interest as my knee was just starting to get better. Falcon's writing went like this:

I am confused.
I don't know what to write
I don't know what to eat
I don't know what to think
I am confused.
My Dad said I had to write this
I don't know why.
Maybe he is confused too.
I don't know. Maybe when I grow up,
I won't be confused
But maybe my confusion will grow up too.

The trip around the North Island of New Zealand was great. Karen had spent the 5 years just before I met her, living in New Zealand. She started out picking fruit and went on to teaching school. By the time she left, she was a department head at the University of Wellington. In her five years, she visited many sights and now she was proudly showing them off to us. It was cool to have your own tour guide. The highlights were climbing Mount Egmont (with Falcon's sparrows), eating corn boiled in volcanic hot springs, seeing the Maori perform their Haka in Rotorua, and a day at a working cattle farm. Falcon loved everything. Even when he was forced to write reports, something he hated and delayed till the last second; he still loved the experience.

His math skills improved as long as he was working one on one. I had trouble with math as a youngster till one day on a golfing outing, my father made a point of adding up his score in his head at the end of each 9 holes. This totally blew my mind. I was used to thinking of math as something that had rigid rules that had to be OBEYed; certainly not something that was good for showing off and getting attention. While obedience was not my trump suit, showing off was. Whenever my family went out for dinner my father gave me the bill to check, mentally. If I found a mistake, I got to keep the money. Needless to say, after that, I put a lot of intention into mental arithmetic. That led to increased ability in all maths. I tried to recreate the same experience for Falcon, but I was less skillful than my old man. Or it could be Falcon doesn't carry my twin curse of disobedience and overconfidence.

New Zealand was great, except for the price of booze. One day, while staring in shock at the beer prices at the store, a little old white haired local lady next to me, said,

"Who can afford those prices? Why don't you brew your own like a Kiwi?" She took me by the hand and showed me where the beer brewing kits were stocked. She gave me a quick 5 minute course in beer making and I returned to the boat loaded with equipment but having forgotten the loaf of bread I was supposed to pick up. Within a month we were beer makers and life was good.

Back on the boat, exploring the seacoast, we were anchored in a tight little bay when a nasty squall blew in. A Kiwi boat came in and anchored way too close to our neighbor. And then he started to drag. The captain of the dragging boat tried to ignore the situation, like it might go away if he didn't acknowledge it. Our neighbor just stood there in his cockpit, smoking his pipe, watching as the new boat slowly dragged to within a few feet of his boat. I couldn't believe my eyes. If that was me I would be jumping around, shouting and screaming and swearing up a blue stump. Our neighbor continued to watch the dragging boat which finally moved after dragging within a foot of his neighbor in 35 to 40 knots of wind.

I was flabbergasted. Our neighbor had behaved with so much class. I remembered a boat in Bora Bora that had anchored 30 feet away, smack in front of me in a very exposed, windy anchorage and then proceeded to leave the boat without even backing down on his hook to set it. Did I ever scream and swear! Not very classy. That day in New Zealand changed my life. I pledged to myself that I would try to be more classy than aggressive. And you know what? I have. All because of one Kiwi who probably never even knew I existed. I talked about it to Falcon, about the lesson I learned. He looked at me as if to say, 'well, yeah.' 'Duh!'

In the Bay of Islands, we stopped at one island that had the best, and I mean the best, green lipped mussels. What we did was, land the rowing dinghy on the beach, walk up this 'hill' (I would have called it a mountain!), skirted the sheep and sheep poop, go back down the other side and stand in the surf line and grab mussels whenever the 10 foot surge went away for a few seconds. After we had our quota we climbed back over the Himalayas and returned to our beach. I was too tired to row back out to the boat and Falcon was too hungry, so Karen cooked them right there on the beach. Man, were they ever good!

Mike building a guitar case into the boat

Educational Experience

Cheep and ReCheep

W e were in the Bay of Islands in the north part of New Zealand on a camping trip when Falcon found 3 baby birds that fell out of their nest. He took them around the campground to see if someone could identify them. The first person he found told him to kill them right away, before they could grow up.

"Those are mynah birds. Look at those yellow legs. Those birds are the worse scourges in New Zealand. Kill them!" Falcon ignored him and promptly named them Cheep, ReCheep and LastCheep.

The baby birds looked so helpless, and depended on Falcon so entirely, that he fell in love with them. We bought him some dry cat food, an eye dropper to give them water and a pair of tweezers to shove the cat kibbles down into their crops. He fed them every hour on the hour, even getting up at night at all hours. He kept them in a shoe box that he held in his arms in his sleeping bag at night. One bird died the first night from injuries from the fall, and that made him want to care for the others even more. He went to a vet who informed him that he was the proud guardian of a pair of sparrows.

We had bought a rolling wreck for $500 NZ, as it was much cheaper way to explore the joys of New Zealand. Falcon set up the back seat as a traveling bird house. When we climbed mountains as part of our trip, Falcon carried his box of birds up and down the trails. As they grew older, they stood on top of the back seat of the car. They were hilarious to watch through the rear view mirror as they swayed this way and that, as we made our way along New Zealand's twisty roads.

Falcon taught them to eat from his lips and they would nibble at his ear, when hungry. After a month, they were flying around the car and then out the windows. Every time we set up camp, they would find a likely tree and settle in for the night. In the morning, they returned to their traveling nest.

After 6 weeks, it was time to leave the nest. One night they didn't return home. Falcon was restless all night and we could hear a few quiet sobs coming from his sleeping bag. The next morning while eating breakfast, Cheep and Recheep flew onto our table. An elated Falcon offered some of his toast but the birds weren't interested. They had friends up in the trees who were telling them in no uncertain terms, that they should wait till the bad people went away before going to the table. Cheep, fat and sassy, flew onto Falcon's shoulder and nibbled at his ear before flying back to the tree. Recheep was soaking wet from a misadventure with a sprinkler, and looked longingly at Falcon before the wildness in her soul made her too, fly away. Falcon again looked so sad and yet happy too, that his friends cared enough to say a final good-bye.

_/) _/) _/)

We sailed up to Whangaparoha.   This was a
beautiful anchorage, fed by a clam filled river and
surrounded by high cliffs. Once, we pulled the dinghy up to
the headwaters to a swimming hole and waterfall. What a
place to enjoy an afternoon, swimming and eating clams.
By the anchorage, a rocky cliff called the 'pope's nose' was
the local rock climbing mecca. Falcon forced us to go with
him to the top, mostly just to watch him jump like a deer
and to applaud at appropriate times. His mother closed her
eyes when he was near the edge. She preferred not to see
him fall to his death. Here was a girl who has sailed
around the world engineless, who swims with and chases
sharks, who fights off pirates, who loves to live up to 6
months at a time like Robinson Crusoe, who delights in
outwitting the Authorities, who has been through countless
hurricanes, who works like a slave and cooks heavenly like
the courtesan she is, who has stared, unflinchingly, into the
eyes of death and laughed, but is scared of a little cliff.
Mothers; go figure!
Eventually the season advanced and hurricane
season drew to its close. It was time to return to sailing.
Karen was desolate. She would be very happy to remain
always in New Zealand but, alas, she might be able to get
me into the country but not the boat. The boat was only
given 6 months, duty free. It was only for her love of me,
that we left together in April, bound towards Brisbane,
Australia. It was a lovely sail for 5 days, and then warnings
of a late hurricane blasted over the airwaves. We didn't
feel too threatened as we were far south and the hurricane
was aiming to go up the Coral Sea. The next day the storm
turned south; just as a precaution we turned south and
headed towards Southport. The next day the storm turned
more south and east! I started to think this storm had our

name written on it. We turned more south and headed towards Lord Howe, a little island in the middle of the Tasman Sea with a marginal anchorage. 'Yali', as it was now called, continued to chase us, but we managed to arrive 24 hours before the storm was due to hit us. At this time it was a category 3 hurricane but was expected to increase to a 4 before a slow death in the cold Southern Ocean. Then, as the forecasters and hurricanes do, they changed their mind again. Now, it looked like it was going to make a direct hit on Lord Howe as a category 5 hurricane. Last time we had had a category 5, we had been in the Virgins in a super protected hurricane hole of an anchorage. This time, we were as exposed as could be, without being at sea.

I found a motel in a well protected valley and we evacuated the boat to move in. Karen was in tears. She caressed everything on her boat. A boat she had helped change from a near derelict to a yacht, and was now abandoning in its moment of greatest danger. Who knew what would be left of her magic carpet in 24 hours. She took a few keepsakes, her marriage license and her engagement ring, and reluctantly half fell in the life boat that had come to rescue us, in tears. There was a dangerous reef on one side 100 feet away and a tall cliff on the other side 120 feet away. We moored the boat to a 10,000 pound destroyer mooring with our strongest lines and hoped for the best. Dragging either way would mean a total loss. Fraying the lines would be a total loss. She only had to slip a boat's length back in almost any direction and we would lose Beau Soleil.

Once we arrived at the hotel, I made a lame excuse about looking for a bakery and went back out to my boat. I couldn't leave her all alone. I wasn't going to let her die without at least trying to save her. I wasn't going to risk my family's life, but I wasn't going to let my boat die with out a fight. I figured that I had a good chance of swimming to safety if Beau was destroyed. Even in the huge seas in the middle of a hurricane I thought I could swim it if I could get enough breath. I was once sunk on a reef in Hawaii while gill netting. I got greedy and was going for Moi, a very valuable fish, and figured I could get in and out between sets of ten foot breakers on the edge of a reef. I figured wrong. It was a dangerous thing to do, as you don't want to get tangled in the net and trapped under water in the surf line. I made it, only breaking one leg, mostly because of St. Jude (a saint I seem to call on often) and a handy life cushion which showed me the way to the surface after each wave tumbled me about. Anyway, I had to trick Karen and Falcon as if they had known I was going to stay with the boat, they would have insisted on staying with me and neither was as strong a swimmer as I.

It was a great hurricane. Another daylight storm. It was one of those times I wished I had a movie camera. The boat was heeling from one gunnel to the other. The wind tore all our new masthead instruments off, long before the cyclones around the eye wall were even close. The numerous bow lines were as tight as iron bars and it was impossible to renew the anti-chafing gear under them. The guy in the boat behind me lost his index finger attempting to slide chafing gear under his anchor line in a brief lull. Too brief, the wind came back in less than a second and instantly amputated his finger. The clouds tore around us; the sea was whiter than the beach. I had to hold my hand over my mouth and nose to create a lee to stop the air from being sucked from my lungs and had to crawl Indian style to get forward to check and pat our bow lines, telling them they were doing a good job. The huge waves that I feared would roll over the reef never had a chance. Their breaking tops were blown flat by the incredible wind as soon as they started to lift. What was left of the seas hit the cliffs with incredible force. They were picked up by the wind and carried bodily over the cliff and onto the island so the ricocheting waves I was worried about never happened. Beau handled it like a champ. She ducked and bobbed around each blow from the storm, instead of taking it on the chin. Her builders must have imbued their knowledge of the sea into her.

Soon the eye passed over us with a beautiful blue sky above; then the winds were back but now blowing over the island first, and then to the now, relatively quiet lagoon. I swam ashore to reassure Karen. Falcon never had any doubt. He was just angry that I hadn't taken him with me. We tumbled our destroyer mooring, moving it about 20 feet, something I still couldn't believe would happen. The storm went on to destroy lighthouses on South Island, New Zealand that had stood for a 100 years. Unfortunately, several boats were lost in Lord Howe's lagoon. We helped rescue one of the boats but the other had gone aground on a world heritage site beach. He was lost save getting a helicopter to lift him off. Certainly, there would be no digging of trenches or cutting of roads on such a pristine area.

As usual, I handled the big things OK but blew it on the little important things. I had cruised the coasts of Australia several times before and never had to get a visa, as the captain of a vessel didn't need one, then. So I didn't apply for one this time either. Wrong. They had changed the rules. Did they ever get mad at me! Karen and Falcon, being Kiwis, didn't need visas, thank goodness. They made a big fuss about throwing me out, but they were just playing the game. I apologized profusely and that was it.

After a while the game of clearing customs becomes a dance, a structured dance where each party follows the same steps. You take the lead and present your papers. They pooh-pooh them. You politely ignore them and look casually out the window and wait. They try to get a rise out of you. But you politely look disinterested. They get tired of trying to push you around and stamp your papers.

You go on to the next office where the dance is repeated. Sometimes, I just wanted to shake them by the shoulders, look them in the eye and say, 'Get a life, Man!' But, of course, that isn't an allowed step in this organized dance and if you don't follow the steps, you can't dance. When we visited India on Tola, I was tired of having to hire agents, and was determined to check in by myself. I signed my name 972 times before I was through. All to save a $25 agent fee! It would have been easier to follow the steps.

The trip towards Southport was uneventful. Nevertheless we kept looking over the other shoulder in case another hurricane was sneaking up on us. Southport is Australia's surfing capital of Queensland. The beaches were full of surfers and we suddenly had bred a surfer dude, it seemed. We were forced to trod to endless surf shops till Falcon found a board to his liking. We split the cost with Falcon, with the understanding that he would pay us back from his earnings.

We didn't pay him an allowance. If he wanted money, he earned it. However, we didn't make earning it difficult. For example, we paid him 5 cents for every fly he killed down below and a penny for every death on deck. I wondered a bit if I was breeding a mercenary and waited to catch him shooing the flies down below where he could increase his profits. He never did. It had to be Karen's good influence!

We didn't pay him for working on the boat. What we did, though, was when something had to be done, everyone worked. This I had learned from my days of long line fishing, one of the most brutal jobs ever. Fishing, we worked 20 hour days of back breaking labor for weeks on end. If there was a job to be done, no matter how small, everyone helped. If someone didn't work, he didn't eat. It was a tough world out there. Falcon excelled at climbing the mast to guide us through the reefs and at raising the anchor. We didn't have a windlass. We raised the anchor with manpower, all of us pulling in unison. The sails, all of us helped to raise. Many hands made a tough job easy. We did offer him an allowance when he turned 8. He wasn't interested. He would rather work as a team, than be paid to do a job alone.

Falcon went out to the big wave beach with his board. I don't think he realized how big the waves were till he looked at them sitting on his board at water level, or how fast they moved. He did catch a couple of waves in the slop before loosing his nerve; to give him credit, he knew first hand just how violent the sea can become. He couldn't pretend to himself that he would be alright. He knew how thin the line between life and death was.

Karen's guitar had broken its neck when it flew out of a locker during Yali. This was the guitar she had played to herself while living in Port Moresby, New Guinea, when her house was surrounded by locals, one night, trying to get in for a bit of the old raping, torturing and killing. She kept her sanity by making up songs and playing them all night long to herself, whilst her doors and windows suffered increasingly violent attacks. Her guitar meant a lot to her. I glued it back together, but Karen said it didn't sound right. As we wandered around looking for surfboards, we also kept a weather eye out for guitars. Finally we found one, a Yamaha, and I built a special locker for this one with a guitar shaped door to keep it safe, just in case we got into another storm.

Our New Zealand school year was drawing to a close. Outside of the country, we had to pay for the shipping for Falcon's work, and we didn't receive his work back till 6 months had passed. Karen was upset. That is just too long, she thought. We had some Wal-Mart school work left and we searched thru used book stores for appropriate school books.

Before us, lay the whole length of the Great Barrier Reef, one of the most exquisite cruising areas ever. This was my third time up the Reef but I was still looking so much forward to it. For Karen, this was her first time in the lower reef and she and Falcon had heard so many tales from my lips that they couldn't wait either. After visiting the International Anchorage in the middle of Brisbane, with the dinghy dock in one of the largest botanical gardens in the southern hemisphere, we zoomed up the Barrier Reef stopping nightly till we arrived at Middle Percy. The Barrier Reef should have been a fringing reef; it was not, because of the itinerant rivers flowing seaward from Queensland's coastal mountains. The fresh water from these rivers killed the inshore coral over many millennia forcing the surviving coral many miles seaward. What were left were some high volcanic and granite islands populating a natural passage between land and reef for 1250 miles up the Australian Coast. We were protected from the Coral Sea and the Pacific swells by the reef. The wind was unabated. We surfed up the reef!

One of these islands, Middle Percy, is heaven on earth. It is a communally held island, with usually just one caretaking family in residence. They grow ducks and pea hens (female peacocks) for their eggs and maintain a veritable garden from which they are happy to sell their products. On the beach is a series of abandoned shacks, decorated with mementos from all the boats that passed this way during the last 150 years. On the trails of the island are thousands upon thousands of butterflies. There are so many you have to wave them away from your face just to see where the path is. The island has a natural harbor on the west side with a drying out grid. This is where we were bound. We had a problem with the cutlass bearing which was hurt from powering full ahead for too long during the worse gusts of Yali, and we had to replace it. The yards, here abouts, were very expensive and anyway who needed them? What with a 20 foot tide? We tied on to the grid. The dock looked a little rickety so we sent hawsers up to the trees as well to be sure Beau wouldn't fall down.

As the tide went out we went to the beach where Karen took a bath in the spring fed, claw footed bath tub sitting in sand in the middle of the beach, while Falcon and I made our memento for the latest shack.

Later when it was Falcon's turn in the bath, (this was his second bathtub bath of his life and he was determined to do it right. He had more bubbles in there than water!) Karen and I climbed up to a huge hammock under the roof of an A-frame shack which led to this and that. We returned to Beau at half tide just in time to see her slowly lean over away from the dock and lay down on her port side in the ebbing water. It was like slow motion. The trees and hawsers slowly stretched, the dock fittings easily broke off and she settled down on the just awash mud without a whimper. It was really funny in a weird psychological way and could have been very dangerous for the boat till we noticed that the mud had been raked clean of any rocks or projections. We weren't the first to lay down in Middle Percy! Until the tide came back up, we were camping, and as evening approached the snake in this Eden came to bite. The beach was infested with voracious sand flies, no-see-ems, no-nos, flying teeth. Thousands of 'em! We barricaded ourselves in Beau, almost upright, and hid behind mosquito screens and nursed our wounds as itchy insanity circled the boat outside.

Two hundred miles of the Whitsunday Islands lay before us. A friend in Brisbane gave Falcon a pellet gun and we practiced shooting on uninhabited beaches below beautiful, goat sculptured islands. Karen and Falcon enlisted me, somewhat unwillingly, on a goat hunt. We all had our weapon of choice. It was great fun running after the fleet goats, well, hobbling in my case. Towards the end, a herd of goats walked right past me, not 10 feet away and I just stared at them in wonder. They were so beautiful. I guess I always had the assumption that animals in nature would be, well, scruffy. These were so beautiful. Karen gave me a very hard time about not killing one.

"You are making dinner tonight, great white hunter."

Each island had its own charm, even the resorts. At one park-like resort we walked around gawking at the tourists. We went past a section of land planted with a variety of fruit trees. I couldn't resist. Karen gave me a dirty look, but still I palla-ed a big papaya! At Mercury Island, we hiked up into the hills to a park which looked out over the expanse of the Reef and along the way discovered our very own Koala Bear sitting in a gum tree, minding his own business, taking a nap. I don't think he appreciated our jabbering and pointing. Unimpressed, he turned his back on us and went to sleep.

Eventually, we arrived at Lizard Island. This is where Captain Cook climbed the highest peak on the island to try to find his way out of this huge reef that had him trapped. Naturally, we had to climb the hill, too. There was a cairn at the top where we added our names to the list of stalwart souls who had followed in Cook's footprints. The view was astounding.

Back on the beach, we visited the oceanographic institute on the island as a field trip for Falcon, and were informed that the corals were going to spawn on this very night. Well! This is something that only happens once or twice a year and here we were on the most perfect island with the healthiest coral on the greatest reef ever, on the right day! We prepared ourselves diligently. As the appointed hour approached we became more and more excited. We all checked our masks and lights carefully. We didn't have dive lights so we put flashlights into doubled zip locks and prayed they wouldn't leak. The institute had told us when the magic hour was and as our timer approached zero we were jumping out of our skins. In the water we went and...! Say What?

On TV, when we watched the spawning of the reefs on the science channel, it was a nice orderly affair. The beautiful peaceful corals gently release a little bubble that one day might be a new coral reef, if it minded his p's and q's. It was all done so properly, almost reverently. Not at all like our experience. Not at all like nature gone mad. They didn't tell us the reef was going to come out and grab us! We weren't prepared for the suddenness of it; the speed, the power, the bursting life of it all.

There we were watching our nice little reef in the beautiful crystal clear water of the outer reef in the light of our flashlights, and then, in seconds, we were surrounded by billions of baby corals. We couldn't even see our hands held in front of our masks! We climbed back into the dinghy and just lay there laughing our fool heads off! I couldn't tell you today why it was so funny, but we have never laughed so hard, ever!

Up in Princess Charlotte Sound, further up the reef, we met a crew of young lobster fishermen. You have to be young to lobster on the upper reef. One of their group turned 18 and they were having a no-holds party to beat all parties. They invited us along and adopted Falcon as a junior tribe member of their group. They had serious pangas (heavy fiberglass work boats) with massive outboards on them. Falcon spent the day ferrying the men around from beach to ship and back, driving these boats with close supervision. They attained speeds of over 50 knots in seconds from a sitting start. It would be awhile till he was satisfied with our little 15 horse outboard again! Karen and I helped cook endless amounts of steaks and shrimp (no lobsters- you never eat the catch) and did our part to go through 3 kegs of beer. The fishermen played keg throw on the beach- seeing who could throw an empty beer keg the farthest. Those boys knew how to enjoy themselves. They had to; they were in a very dangerous profession.

We were now in the waters of the Salties. These were the big, up to 24', salt water crocodiles that roam as much as 100 miles out to sea. They were very dangerous animals. And smart? Watch yer back, mate, they'll sneak up and grab a bite, fair dinkum; especially if you are searching for lobster instead of keeping an eye out for danger. If that wasn't enough, we were now in the area of box jellyfish. These little buggers are almost invisible and like to live in the shallow water by beaches. They are so poisonous that one touch, unless neutralized immediately, burns right through your leg to the bone and the flesh will never, ever heal for the rest of your life. And that is if you neutralize it quickly; if you don't, within 60 seconds you are dead. If that wasn't enough, this was the region for blue ring octopus. These shy guys will kill you in 30 seconds. If that wasn't enough, now we started to see sea snakes. They only have little mouths but if they can bite you on the nose or lips or little toes, you will want to die as quickly as you can, so bad is the pain. All of the above convinced us that swimming was on hold for the duration. We always carried ammonia or vinegar in the dinghy and jumped from the bow to the sand to go ashore. Even when we threw a bucket into the sea to throw over ourselves to cool off we took a real close look first for any bad things lurking inside.

After Thursday Island, at the top of the reef, we stopped at Gove where we were married years ago. 'Jump up', one of the kid boats from the South Pacific, joined us after Karen told them what a great place it was on the radio, and we buddy boated together over to Darwin. The kids played together constantly. When they became bored with our adult talk, they went below and joined together to beat educational software games. Falcon would navigate the hero through mazes while older Eileen would solve math problems while much younger Greg would handle everything else. Once Falcon surfaced from the forepeak and asked,

"When are you dolts going to eat?" He was greeted with four pairs of eyes in stony silence. "Well, each of you is an a-dult, aren't you?" Why, can't they stay small and cute? Wait, don't answer that. Someone has to support us in our old age!

We sailed together across the top to Darwin. The wind was light so much of the time that we raced each other flying spinnakers and drifters. It was a good time. Often we switched crew to experience sailing on a different boat and to take pictures of our own. Rather than complain about the lack of wind and end up motoring the last 300 miles, we created many memories to last a life time.

Karen's Coconut Crab

RETURN TO CHAGOS

The fleet splits again after Darwin. Some go to Christmas and Cocos Keeling and hence on to Mauritius, South Africa and the Cape. Some go on to Sri Lanka, I've Had Enough of You, and the Red Sea. Others, who thought ahead and were rich enough to buy a cruising permit 6 months in advance from Indonesia, (and it actually arrived in Darwin in time), headed up to Bali, Singapore, Malaysia and Thailand. We didn't have the extra whatever hundreds of dollars it is this year for a cruising permit, but I didn't think that should stop us. Were we out here living a life of freedom, or what? It wasn't like we were going to cruise the country or anything. Just stop at a few places for the fun of it. Just to get the taste of the country. Yeah, that's right. Sure. I might even believe it.

The first place we stopped was on the north side of Bali. Almost all boats stop in the south, at Benoa, the harbor for Denpasar on the south coast of Bali. We anchored off of Singaraja, where the mayor came out in response to our Quarantine flag. I explained that I had a bad heart and needed a couple days of rest and we would move on. He seemed fine with that. Karen was not. She was sure I had crossed my stars and I would drop dead from a heart attack at any moment. After reprovisioning at cheap but poorly stocked grocery stores we carried on to Borneo and the Kumai River. Borneo has several sanctuaries for wild orangutans and one of them was on a tributary off the Kumai River and it was on our way, kind of, as we headed north towards Thailand. I sent Karen ashore to handle the authorities since she disagreed with my last effort.

I don't know how that girl does it. She took Falcon with her as he was going through a 'cute' stage and marched up to the first soldier she found, stared him down, and stated she was going to see the wild orangutans. That got her to the head man who wanted to see her cruising permit. She told him she didn't want to cruise Indonesia; just to see the orangutans. They stared at each other, till he looked down first, he looked up again and angrily told her it would cost extra. She smiled and started bargaining. Three hours later she returned to the boat. We were set. She had organized for a guard for Beau while we were gone, a launch and driver to take us up the skinny little river to the Sanctuary, food for us and our driver for the 3 days the trip would take, and made the Authorities happy, all for $50 American. I guess it pays to have a Masters Degree in Counseling!

What a great experience. On the way up the little river, monkeys would swing across the water, the little babies would hang onto their moms and swim across trying to catch up with their big brothers, gavials (the third and largest of the crocodile-alligator family) peered at us from the weeds, thousands of birds flew over us when disturbed, and when anchored for the night we ate dinner by the light of billions of fireflies in the trees. Our driver was great. He would stop the boat in the middle of the river and just point. At first we didn't see anything but with time we made out animals hiding in the over-hanging trees. We visited several orangutan camps. It turned out the major effort of these camps was to rehabilitate orangutans that had been in captivity, mostly in bars, to the wild existence. Every month they would feed the animals deeper and deeper in the woods. We were met at the docks by a biologist who took us for a tour and explained their efforts. At one camp the biologist was late. We hung around the dock waiting for him to show up. One lady orangutan took a liking to me after she checked me out by sliding her hand deep into my front pocket to make sure I was suitably equipped! On the way to the feeding station the little orangutans tried to get a ride on one of us rather than walk, which was totally against the rules. They were supposed to be learning to survive on their own. Karen refused to pick up a little one which Falcon ended up carrying, which made her jealous. Girls, damn but they are hard to figure out!

Back on Beau, we anchored at Bintan, in the north of Indonesia, and stared at wonder at the traffic going through the Singapore Straights. The ships seemed endless. They were all motoring at flank speed because of the danger of pirates. There were 4 different shipping lanes through the 10 mile strait, each with two way traffic and we had to get through them! The wind was in our favor, we raised every sail we had and we revved the engine up to maximum and went for it.

I have to admit I was nervous but Falcon was looking at me with all the confidence in the world so I just had to act like I knew what I was doing. We dashed under one freighter's stern, got out of his wake and tried to get in front of the next ship in line. Often we had to duck under his stern, too. If this kept up, we would be in Thailand before we were through the shipping lane! Eventually we made it and to celebrate we stopped at a marina in

Malaysia. Asia is the last great place for impoverished sailors. Marinas, food, booze, restaurants, everything is cheap. Our marina cost us $50 American for a week and included a swimming pool with its own waterfall and a free shuttle in a hydrofoil to Singapore.

Dear Reader and Fellow Adventurer, I know you consider America and Europe as the first world, but it isn't so. Sorry to have to break it to you like this. We are the second world, Singapore is the first. Sorry, I know it is a disappointment, but it's true. Remember when 1984 came and went and we all looked around and asked where 'Big Brother' was? We got, in a weird way, disappointed and all? I got news for you. He came. He is alive and well in Singapore. Think of all the problems 'first world' cities have. Singapore has solved them all. True, civil liberties became financial liabilities. You can do what ever you want, just get ready to be fined for it. Oh, they won't catch you? Sorry, you have already deposited your fine to the government ahead of time, just in case. For example, traffic problems. Every car has a little chip that tells 'big brother' which street it is on. The busier streets cost more money to drive on than the vacant ones. Once you use up the money deposited to 'B. B.' your car stops and won't start until you pay more money. You are free to honk your horn as much as you wish, you are charged for each honk. If you make an illegal turn? Or run a red light? Yes, that's right; the money is deducted from your account within seconds. I know I don't have to tell you, the more fines you incur, the higher the rate they are taken from you.

However, the monorails are fast and quick and cheap. Of course, you can't chew gum anywhere in Singapore as you might spit it out and slow down the monorails. Lest you think it is all bad, any high-rise being built also has to build its own septic system, its own schools and it must also build 5 times the footprint of its high-rise in parks. There are so many parks on that island; it is like living in Disneyland with double the crowds. That's the problem. Singapore is an island with nowhere to build except up. Sooner or later every city will have that challenge too.

Karen hurt her foot walking around the parks at our marina in Malaysia. She thought it was broken. We asked at the front desk for a doctor.

"Yes, no problem, good Chinese doctor here. He will break it the other way." We thought she was joking. When we got to the doctor he strapped her leg to the table and was starting to break it the other way when Karen screamed bloody murder. I think I have related that it is wise to always stay on Karen's good side. I didn't realize how right I was till I saw the quivering wreck of what was left of the doctor when Karen was through with him! I don't want to give the wrong impression. Karen is very meek and mild. She is grace personified. She is the perfect wife and first mate/co-captain. But please, be kind to yourself, don't get her blood up.

Off we went to Singapore on the ferry. We stopped at the first clinic we came to. She was x-rayed, MRI-ed, every kind of -eyed; she had a bad sprain. Cost for the doctor? $20 American. Karen had some skin cancer and went to the skin cancer clinic in Singapore. She had 10 spots removed and her entire body examined under a magnifying glass. $50 American and it was that much just because every six months you paid another $50 American ahead of time just to make sure you came in to get checked as you had already paid for it. You could go as often as you wanted, as long as you didn't mind standing in line. Of course don't try to cut ahead in line. That's right, another fine. There is a great T-shirt. 'Singapore is a fine city,' and goes on to list the many fines, tourists can be charged for.

We went to the night zoo which was way different. Many of the animals in zoos are sleeping when we see them during the day as they are nocturnal. At the night

188

zoo these animals came alive. Many of the non-dangerous animals were let loose and wandered about the paths and roads. But the predators! For the first time I understood what Blake meant when he wrote, 'Tiger, Tiger, burning bright!' I shivered in my shoes as the caged tiger sized me up for a snack and licked his chops. Falcon stared nonstop at a Bengal for 3 minutes straight through a big glass wall. Finally the big cat couldn't take it anymore and with a huge leap crashed into the glass pane. I sure was glad it was strong enough! The fishing cats were the best. They looked like your normal pet cat but they sneaked up on a small pond, spotted a fish in the water below and launched themselves legs spread into the pond with a big splash. Quickly they pulled their stunned fish out of the water, ate it up and then did it all over again. They didn't seem at all concerned with their wet fur.

We left Singapore bound thru the Straits of Malacca, home of the pirates. We worried about anchoring out at night. It wasn't a place to sail at night, as we found out, after we ran into a submerged banana tree, not a frond, the whole tree and got it fouled in our propeller. It turned out the pirates, as was the case in the Red Sea, weren't interested in us. The big ships carried their own payrolls in their safes and at times transported gold. Once we were sure we saw pirates as they raced at high speed right past us heading out to a solitary freighter. They waved their AK-47s and smiled as they passed!

Our first anchorage was on an offshore island. Falcon stood guard with his little pellet gun till he got tired about 9 PM. The only ones who passed were fishermen who waved cheerfully and continued on their way. Our next stop was on an island off the town of Lumut. We walked through the town and had a great time. The yacht club was friendly; Kentucky Fried Chicken and McDonalds were everywhere. By the harbor was a rock walk. The Muslims believe that if you walk barefooted over upturned rocks, they will massage your feet and keep your body in good working order. The rocks were cemented in place to be sure to keep the pointed end up.

It took one circle to convince Falcon and I that one had to be a fanatic to do it more than once. Karen kept going around with the locals dressed in black with only their burning eyes showing. She and one man raced side by side. Neither would quit first. Karen made it around 5 times before quitting. Her antagonist quit just after her. For the next week she couldn't walk, her feet were so swollen. She might be a fanatic but, you know what? She is our fanatic.

We kept looking for the pirates. Everyone talks about them. We were sure they must be here somewhere. We eventually found them.

Malaysia is a very Muslim country so they try to limit their citizens' exposure to 'evil' tourists by isolating them, the tourists that is. The way they handled cruising boats is they made one of the many offshore islands duty free for everything. Plus they built modern marinas available for a pittance. Needless to say we, as well as every cruising boat in the area, headed straight for our newest Eden. Langkawi lived up to its billing. It had it all, crystal clear lakes in ancient volcanoes, modern shopping at last century's prices (I mean, European beers at less than $5 American a case!), cheap restaurants, artwork everywhere, eagles flying over head, and lots of laughing fellow rovers.

One of the fancy stores had a big sale of Malaysian crafts to lure people in. It had a blow pipe target practice contest with a hundred Ringgit prize. Whenever we walked by, Falcon and I would go in the store and get in a bit of practice. When the big day came you know who the big winner was? No, not us. They brought in a ringer from Borneo who swept the competition. We did come first in the tourist class and got a neat little dust collector.

Christmas time was coming and we planned to fly back to California to visit my mother. One of the lures for making the flight was my mother had met a school teacher at the local grade school. It seems that book publishers send out sample books each year to every school in the land. If the teachers are not interested in that volume for the upcoming school year they place it in a magic place called the TRR. TRRs are the cruising family's dream come true. The Teacher Resource Room contains hundreds of books for each grade level that will never be used. My mother's friend was more than willing to supply us, free of charge, with a huge box for each grade level for the rest of Falcon's grade school education. Falcon was under whelmed, to say the least. He took one look at the huge pile of books he was supposed to read for the coming years and left for a two hour walk!

We discovered Malaysia had an interesting idea about copyright laws. They felt they would start obeying them when they had pulled their country up by the boot straps, out of the Stone Age and into the First (second) World. Every kind of software was pirated. AHA! At last we found the Pirates of the Malacca Straits! Anyway, we paid pennies on the dollar. Karen was upset about the whole affair. She firmly believed in laws and right and wrong. Me? I had spent my life being taught by the sea that it is always better to dodge than take it on the chin. For me, corners were for going around. Straight lines were for Saints and those lacking imagination, especially when the software could help my son. They offered thousands of titles in educational software ranging from math, to history, to foreign languages, to English, all for two bucks a piece. Falcon took a look at the stuff I brought home and started hating everything to do about school.

In Malaysia he flat out went on strike. He buried his huge pile of school books and software under his pillow and declared he was going to learn 5th grade through osmosis. He refused to write letters. He refused to write anything. There was no reasoning with him. We tried everything to make him see the light. Nothing worked. So I decided to write a book.

In Asia, he borrowed our dinghy and spent every day ferrying sailors from the docks to their boats and back again. In Langkawi he made a deal with the resort icemaker people and sold ice that he delivered to yachts. He enlisted all his little friends to help him out as his business grew. He fixed up a discarded bike to get his ice delivered faster. That kid loved making money. He hated spending it, but he sure loved making it. It took two books to get him turned around. The first was a collection of essays on the strange philosophy of long term sailors, "The Tigers Will Eat You Alive". The second was the "Hong Book." Hongs are fantastic limestone 'caves' in islands, in Thailand above Phuket, that have a lake inside and a collapsed roof, that used to make it a true cave. They are like returning to the world of Jurassic Park. It is hard to believe such beauty can exist in our rough old world without someone collecting money at the entrance. There were many cruising guides on Thailand and Malaysia, none made but a passing comment on the hongs. I sensed a market here. I talked Falcon into selling my books, boat to boat as it were. I hoped that he would see that there was money in the ability to write; that there was value in learning.

Eventually his mother had a heart to heart with him and he went back to studying. He complained that all the other boat kids had less work to do than he. It didn't do any good to remind him that he was at least a year older than most, unfortunately the only kid older than he had abandoned school; it was too much trouble for his parents to teach him, apparently, and he did poorly learning by himself. He spent his time swimming in the resort pool and surfing off the beach. (He ended up years later captaining racing boats.)

To solve the problem, Karen let Falcon set his own school hours and subjects. He really liked history. His mother, who took math as a minor in college, encouraged him strongly to include math as a subject. It was his decision. He assigned himself a creative writing course. (Aha! Success!) He had a list of a dozen books he said he would read and do reports on, and he set himself to complete a comparative reading course. He studied typing, spelling and math on the computer with various games we had found. In short, he assigned himself more work than we would have given him!

He did great. He completed 3 years of history text books in one year. It really helped that we had encyclopedias on the laptop, (Hey, for a few dollars, how could we not?), so he could continue to explore timelines that interested him. Along with his school reading he devoured popular fiction, (Mostly Clive Cussler and Michael Crichton.) Any adventurous book that I recommended was on his extracurricular list as long as it didn't look like a school book. He still waited till the last second of the last day to write his reports. We bought a typing game, that he topped out at 70 words, error free, per minute, much, much faster than his old man.

Part of his renewed enthusiasm was we were preparing to sail out to Chagos. This was a British Territory where they had thrown all the locals out to turn Diego Garcia into a major naval base. Once, it was a lot nicer. When I first visited in the late 70's on Time Out, I sailed right into Diego Garcia, tacking this way and that, as I was engineless, looking for a place to anchor. There were scores of ships anchored in the lagoon which made it hard to see the land. I think everyone thought I was some Captain's toy boat lowered off his ship. No one bothered me. Finally after I anchored I was suddenly surrounded by

20 swift boats all pointing their .50 caliber machine guns at me. With a lot of quick talking, they let me stay; my port spreader was slightly bent so they dropped my mast and rewelded the whole thing; I was short of groceries so they loaded me up with 3 gigantic cardboard boxes of food and liquor. On the last day the Commander came down and accused me of planning to stop at their lagoon. I said no, no, my boat was wounded, I had to stop. He threw 2 letters from my French girl friend addressed to Port Captain, Diego Garcia at me and told me to get out. Since then the navy's reception of visiting yachtsmen at Diego Garcia has been less than welcoming. Sorry, guys.

Anyway, we were still allowed to visit the three other lagoons in the group. The fishing was first rate, the islands were vacant and loaded with fruit, the beaches were as white as they came and the parties on the beach were legendary around the world. To prepare to go to the islands required a different set of tools than those we would normally carry. It was great fun stocking up with shovels, machetes, saws and ladders. Falcon saw in his mind the biggest tree fort since Swiss Family Robinson that he and his cronies were going to build. He was jumping out of his skin with excitement!

Two weeks into departure preparations I announced that we couldn't go. Falcon hadn't been keeping up with his school work, what with all his architectural designs of tree forts, and I said I was thinking of sending him back to the US for boarding school. The drama! The yelling! The horror! I stuck to my guns and suddenly we had the most studious student in the world. He even wrote his reports on the second to the last day!

On the way towards Sri Lanka, Karen became very sick. She had problems years ago with a cyst on her ovary and she thought this was the same pain. It got worse and worse. She couldn't eat. She could barely drink water and then only in tiny sips. On arrival in Galle, I rushed her over to the hospital and ran into a brick wall. They wanted no part of a white woman. In the past, every time they opened up a white woman, she died in days and in incredible pain. They didn't have the resistance to all the different germs that would invade their system in such a basic hospital.

My poor Karen sat on a dirty wooden stool in the waiting room, in agony, whist she was ignored by doctors and nurses. She normally weighed 130 pounds and now after a week at sea in agony she was down to 105. I left the hospital and rushed to every drug store in town looking for something that might help. When I returned. I hardly recognized Karen. The pain had creased and shrunken her face; she was bent over like a hunchback and couldn't straighten herself. I mixed her a cocktail of the most potent of the muscle relaxants I had found and forced it down her throat. I carried her outside to a bench where the air was fresher and she could watch the setting sun as I held her in my arms. She was as light as a feather. I brushed her hair and rubbed her back as the tears ran down my face. I held her twisted body up so we could watch what might be our last sunset together. Finally the medicine started to work. Inch by inch she started to relax. After four hours on our park bench she finally was able to sit up. That night I brought her home to Beau and Falcon, where she made a complete and total recovery. I don't know what was in those pills but I still have some just in case!

Off we went towards the Maldives. I tried to talk Karen into returning to Singapore where at least they had first world hospitals, but she wouldn't hear of it. She wanted to go to Chagos, no matter what. If she was going to die she wanted to see Chagos first.

The Maldives were great. They were building up their islands as the ocean waters rose, world wide, with banks of cement and rebar. They stacked up the cement bags on the edge of the water at low tide and drove rebar thru the bags and into the coral below. As the tide rose the water set the cement and a seawall, however weak, was formed in a day. It was something only desperate people would do, but then their homeland is disappearing into the rising sea and they are desperate indeed. Soon we were off towards Chagos. Finally we were on our way; we were on the last lap. We were almost there!

How can one describe perfection? How can a writer relate perfect happiness? Is it even possible? Four months later we were still in Chagos and only then preparing to leave as we had no sugar, flour, veggies, coffee, eggs, milk, canned food, propane for the stove or gas for the outboard left. We kept putting off departing till we really had to leave. We couldn't tear ourselves away from paradise. Lots of fish, lobsters, coconuts, and breadfruit got us to the Seychelles. What happened in-between? It was all a blur. The high points: wild parties on the beach, endless hours snorkeling in crystal clear water and swimming thru gigantic schools of fish, helping Falcon with his school work and tree forts, trolling for wahoo and mahi, spear fishing coral trout and grouper, drying fish only to turn around to find Falcon had eaten it all while still wet, scaring ourselves silly when Falcon was attacked by a shark, spending days beachcombing around the islands gathering tons of junk that we buried after show and tell, going on coconut crab hunts, making love by moonlight on the foredeck where the water was so clear and the stars reflected so perfectly on the flat sea that it seemed Beau was suspended in space, covered with pixie dust on the way to never-never land. It was a return to childhood and summer vacation again. Every morning we woke with joy and anticipation surging thru our blood as we greeted the day. Every night we fell asleep tired but sated with the happiness of a day well spent just messing about.

In Chagos, for biology, Falcon and I collected ten Queen Conch. We released them by our anchor and every day swam around, finding each one and recording the distance each covered. After a week, the conch became quite clever at hiding. I don't think they appreciated being transported back to the same batch of sand each day. After two weeks they became so smart we lost them all. Did we create a species of super conch? Biologists, I know Conch are only supposed to exist in the Atlantic and certainly not in the Indian but believe me, given enough time in the Bahamas and Caribbean, one knows his conch and these were conch. We found a lot of unreported species. We left them to grow in peace. Karen and Falcon put their conch data into a report and displayed our findings in a number of mathematical studies. For me, mostly, it was a lot of fun searching for conch everyday.

It was a sad day indeed when we left Chagos, but hurricane season was coming and we were out of food. The good part was everyone else was leaving too, and we returned to our habit of Pacific type nets each morning on the radio. The boats heading down to Madagascar were getting pounded, that's why we chose to go to the Seychelles, that and the fact that they are some of the most beautiful islands in the world.

It was an easy 7 day passage towards the Seychelles. We anchored off a little island with some kids about Falcon's age inhabiting it. Falcon and Dominic got along famously. They got along so well we signed Falcon up to go to Dominic's school for two weeks. Falcon seemed to find these fast and firm friends all around the world. Well, the world he grew up in is one of making new friends in every port. For him it was normal to find long lost brothers in the far corners of the Seven Seas. We went to parent night at Falcon's temporary school. His teachers were impressed with his range of knowledge, sure, but mostly with his insight into problems of the world. His view, from the level of a deck in working ports was much different than viewing it from a 20 story tourist hotel window over looking beautiful scenery empty of people. He grew up seeing the world as it really was, practical and a little dirty; the tourist kids saw an illusion that was created just for them.

Soon again it was time to carry on. The Seychelles were still in the hurricane belt and all our buddies told us how cheap it was down south, so off we went to Mayotte in the Comores, just to the west of Northern Madagascar. Mayotte is one of the last bastions of the French Foreign Legion in Africa. Every day they ran up and down the beach singing their little French songs and saluting their adopted flag. We were surprised to discover that no one in the French Foreign Legion was French. That was why it was called Foreign, I guess. Mayotte was a bit of Paris in the outback. The bakery, after months in Chagos, was heaven on earth! For us Mayotte was a great staging point for Madagascar, our next great adventure.

Nosy Be is an island just off Northern Madagascar. It is the center of cruising in this part of the world. The island itself, while very pretty, pales compared to the islets and anchorages in the area. It has the town and the supplies for those spending more than a few days in the area. Madagascar is wild and jungle filled, while Nosy Be is as civilized as only the French know how. Beautiful cultured plantations fill the country side, pleasant bistros line the beaches. Across the water, 10 miles away, the dark and steamy jungle awaits, filled with all manner of wild creatures. The best were the lemurs. The tame ones, next to the huts, loved to jump down on our shoulders and see if they could get something to eat. They were so light and soft it was like a fly landing instead of a fairly large animal, as big as a large cat. The boat boys came out of tiny tributaries, in dugouts filled with veggies, fruits and nuts to trade for whatever you might have. Karen tried to trade some of my old T-shirts to no avail. They had to be newish!

We stopped in Russian Bay where years ago some Russian sailors did a Mr. Christian on their Soviet Overlords, complete with the sinking of their ship to avoid being found by satellite. Alas, it ended the same, in bloodshed, over women mostly. By the time we got there they were all dead, except for the last 3 that were found and returned to the USSR in chains. The only sign left of them were the little blond kids running around! Here we had a birthday for Falcon under a huge tree on the beach. Fifteen boats showed up for the party mostly because they couldn't believe how we caught our giant Spanish mackerel for the main course. We were just sitting around, working on the boat, when this huge fish jumped 20 feet in the air, going after bugs or whatever, and landed on our deck. The whole boat shook with his efforts to jump back into the water. Falcon and I managed to subdue him. What a feast! To make matters more astounding, another big fish did the exact same thing the next week. Everyone wanted our GPS coordinates so they could anchor in the same spot after we left!

Further south, we sailed into Honey River. There was a school on the south bank of the river that we forced Falcon into going to see. We wanted him to realize how lucky he was to be home schooled on his own boat. We want that knowledge to be guttural, felt in his guts, not just in his head. He kept telling us,

"Hey, I know. I got it, already. Lesson learned. End of story." We made him go anyway!

We came to this river for the honey. It was a dollar a liter but you had to supply your own container and not complain about the odd bee or comb floating around inside. I wish I could tell you what kind of honey it was, certainly not clover, but no doubt it came from flowers of plants not yet discovered. We bought 10 liters and wished we had bought more when we had to return to normal store bought honey. It was that good.

We ran back towards Mayotte which I used to like. There were a lot of boats there, so I was stupid and anchored out towards the end of the group. That night I heard a commotion on a French boat with lots of shouting and yelling involved. I sat up on deck and watched for a few minutes and then like a fool, I went back to bed. That night our beloved Caribe dinghy was stolen. In the morning the painter was cut. We made a fuss but it was never found. No doubt the engine was taken and the dinghy sunk to hide the evidence. We were heart broken.

The hurricane season was almost upon us so we ran up to Tanga in Tanzania which is hurricane free that time of year. What a great spot. We anchored by the yacht club just around from the bay's entrance and had a great seat when the big trading dhows came in the bay. The entrance was reef strewn with cross currents so these 70 foot engineless dhows with a sail well over 100 feet high, surfed into the entrance at speeds exceeding 20 knots. After clearing the reefs, they dropped their sail and coasted the mile and a half to the town docks. The wind thrumming in the sail, the men singing in unison as they readied the anchor and handed the sail, the water being ripped apart by the sharp, flaring bow, the smell of the cargo of cloves, cinnamon and other spices, these are memories not easily forgotten. This is the way of sail now forgotten in our modern world, to our loss.

We met some forestry workers from Finland who were guiding reforestation attempts in Tanzania. They took us on Safari. Not your normal safari, mind you, a local's safari. Once we came upon a pride of lions at a kill and Veli and Rita drove right up to them till we were 20 feet away, across a little creek. Other safari vehicles were there too but they were way back behind trees 500 feet away. Karen, of course, climbed half out of the window for better pictures. This, we later found out was an incredibly stupid thing to do as while the lionesses do the killing, the lion does the protecting. And they don't like people in jeeps sticking their arms out, much less their bodies. We got busted for going too close to the lions, passports seized, (hey, I thought that only happens on boats!) but Veli talked our way out of trouble.

We camped out on the veldt in tents, instead of in secure lodges. One night elephants walked thru our campsite knocking trees down here and there. (Veli told us they don't step on tents. We decided in the interests of sanity, to believe him.) In the mornings we walked thru the veldt like explorers of old, noting hyena spoor 20 feet from the tents. We stared down a rhino going about his own business when we rounded a big tree and came face to face with him, something Veli later told me never, ever to do again.

Often we had to back down trails when rogue elephants made it clear that this was their road. Period. We stopped at a roadside shack and had kudu burgers. You will never eat beef again after you try kudu. It is really, really good.

In Tanga we discovered the local, fell-off-the-truck food store, you know the one, the food pre-cooked it is so hot, and restocked the boat for pennies on the dollar. On Sundays we sailed to the sandbar where the club had its full moon Sunday tea. We got there at low tide and helped set up. We all made a lot of food for this potluck and ate it in style. When the sand bar sunk under the approaching high tide it was the signal to return to the mainland. It was fun to see these proper Europeans in three piece suits take off their shoes and wade out to the launch!

We decided to return to Chagos and to do it right this time. We bought every kind of tool we found we needed last time. We seriously stocked up the boat. We tied 50 extra gallons of diesel and gasoline to the hand rails on deck. But we were too far south to catch the South West Monsoon that we needed to return to our paradise. So up we sailed towards Kilifi in Kenya. This was a beautiful bay north of Mombasa and unlike Mombasa, shark free. They had a sailing camp, while we were there, for all the rich kids down in the big city. At least in Kilifi they could capsize without being eaten! We signed Falcon up and he had a great time playing with all the English speaking kids.

We anchored in front of the local Ham Radio Operator's house. He opened his house to us and we used his beach for landing the dinghy and his boat shed for our shower. Tony's beach was a shark tooth beach. With close attention, one can locate the teeth of extinct species of sharks some of them quite large. The local kids came down to the beach to look for teeth to sell to the tourists and to talk to Falcon. I bought Falcon a Massai bow and arrow. These guys are totally lethal with these little crooked arrows and us guys figured we could be too.

Karen found out all of the ins and outs of British society in Kenya when playing bridge. She played with 3 older women well into their 70's who had spent their whole lives in East Africa. They were overjoyed. Finally someone to talk to who had not heard their stories a thousand times before. They each supported some of their worker's kids in school for which they received fruit or veggies at a time of plenty.

Soon we were back at sea and after a quick stop at the Seychelles, we arrived at Chagos again. What a relief! Gone were the problems of the modern world, gone was trying to find a bus and dealing with the 20 people crowded into the VW van half of whom you knew had HIV. Gone was dealing with the realities of life. We were back in Never-Never Land and life couldn't be better!

Karen and her Guitar Locker

Educational Experience

African Students

It was in Kilifi, Kenya where we first discovered the African desire for education. We were anchored below Tony's house as people did in those days. He hired locals to work around his grounds and if they couldn't get a day's work with Tony they migrated down to the beach to see if anything was happening. Occasionally Karen would hire one of the boys to help with the laundry.

I bought Falcon a Massai bow and arrows for his birthday and as a reward for doing well in school. The Massai bow and arrows look nothing like those we know from Robin Hood and cowboy and Indian movies. There is no fetching on the arrow and the arrow resembles a stick that has been twisted and tortured to have as many curves in it as possible. If there is an opposite to the straight and narrow it is the Massai arrow. It is shot by a little short bow that looks like a toy bow we would give a young boy. The thing was that the Massai were totally deadly with this inadequate looking equipment, able to bring down the biggest game with a single shot and no, it wasn't poisoned.

They could hit the jugular on a charging animal 9 times out of ten.

Falcon and I were determined to learn to shoot the Massai bow and when he tired of pre-algebra and writing book reports, we went to the beach and shot at coconuts much to the amusement of the local boys. It seemed one didn't aim as much commune with the arrow before even notching it; very frustrating. Falcon would ask why the boys weren't in school.

"We want to go to school but we don't have a pencil." Falcon being the trader started accumulating carvings for the pencils he brought from the boat. The older boys had a more serious problem. From third grade on a student had to have shoes. We dragged Falcon to visit the school, a hike of 3 hours. He said he knew he was lucky; he didn't need more evidence of the same but sometimes a visceral experience stays longer than a mental lesson. The children were impeccably dressed with not only shoes but pressed shirts and pants. We could only imagine the effort it took to heat the iron over a wood fire to press those clothes every morning. The teachers were adamant about the shoes requirement.

"There are so many children who want to go to school so desperately but there is no room. If they can't afford a pair of shoes how will they afford the tuition? A family working a field can only afford to send one child to school so they pick the most hopeful one. Maybe if that child is bright he or she may be able to go on to high school and to get a good job in a town." It was true, one of the first questions a kid would ask in Africa was what grade did we get to in school. When we told them of our university experience they could only look in wonderment. It took away the sting of the difference in wealth between living in a grass hut and on a yacht. Instead of seeing us as being rich, they saw us as educated. Their parents saw our life style as a function of education leading to wealth.

Their proudest moment was when a child graduated from primary school. If one got through secondary they were ecstatic, they had someone to support them in their old age. Just attending one year of college was an almost impossible dream. We ended up paying for one kid's schooling. He was a nice, bright boy and his parents were desperately poor.

We never could hit our stationary coconut with our bow and arrow farther away than 20 feet. Maybe some things have to be inherited or learned in the crib.

WHALE ATTACK

Chagos was so great. The clarity of the water and the brilliancy of the sand beneath added to the illusion of floating in mid air. Sometimes, ready to jump off the boat for a swim, we would stop ourselves with the thought 'That is a long, long way to the ground.' Falcon, 12, and a seventh grader was unbelievably happy. He had kept his eyes and ears open last year in Chagos and this time he was ready. When various boats organized 'cook offs' amongst the yachts in residence, where the biggest prize was reserved for bread making, he and Karen each won once. And I wasn't even a judge! Falcon generated a whole new style of bread making, building his own oven from a 3 gallon biscuit tin with holes strategically placed to reinforce the wind over the wood coals to give a fast high heat. He baked his bread in empty bean cans. (No washing up after!) The loaf curled over the top like a big muffin. Was it ever good!

Karen's personal log was filled with entries describing in detail all the recipes she tried. She developed separate ways to cook each of the many species of fish we caught to bring out the best in each dish. Falcon kept a detailed log book of each fish he caught presenting information for species, length, weight, time of day, percent of sky cloudiness, and type and color of lure.

The most common question Karen was asked is, 'What do you do with all your spare time?' The only fair answer is, 'What spare time?' True, compared to a house, there was little housework, but a lot of her day in Chagos was taken up with long walks on deserted beaches, rescuing turtles trapped when the tide went out, gathering breadfruit and millionaire's salad, keeping up with the social complications of a fleet of individualists, keeping the sharks at bay when us men went spearing, long afternoons making love and watching her child erupt into the man he was meant to be. Karen started a garden for her veggies. She grew tomatoes, peppers, green onions and lettuce on her foredeck. We weren't allowed to go sailing unless we gave the farmer 30 minutes warning to lash down her plants. But it was never like living ashore. There was no timetable. Nothing had to be done at a certain time. When an urge manifested itself, we followed it. If we felt like reading a book all day we did. If Falcon and I felt like playing computer games all day we did. No sweat. No blame. We each followed our own agenda. Chagos was so great.

Other boats followed the same unstructured life in Chagos. Some developed their own hydroponic gardens. A fellow cruiser had brought a live chicken down from the Maldives. It was named 'Dinner' as the plan was to eat her after she stopped laying eggs. As they had two pre-teens on board and the chicken became a pet, that day never happened. Chagos was a great place for kids. How could it not be?

There were a lot of young kids but the ones who enjoyed Chagos the most were the teens and pre-teens. Their parents gave them unparalleled freedom as there was no danger from outsiders and everyone knew all the kids. They could run as wild as they wanted in the freedom of an unbelievably beautiful paradise. The adults had parties on the beach or on the boats most every night, around which the 10 to 16 year olds orbited. They appeared periodically to stock up on snacks and then disappeared to endeavors of their own. The younger children played within sight of the adults.

Once a boat ran aground and it took the whole fleet working together to get him off. The only damage was scratches in the paint on the port side. We met him again, years later, and he hadn't fixed his hull paint. When we asked him why, he said,

"I left it like this just to remind myself of how lucky I am to have known such a great bunch of people."

An Indonesian fishing boat ran aground while poaching and the crew escaped on a sister ship before the Brits showed up, leaving a boat full of supplies. We all filled our diesel tanks, we had lots of rice and if we had needed it, we could have had miles of long line. I grabbed a battery off the ship and Falcon collected short pieces of line that he traded for important kid stuff over the next couple of years. It was a godsend to a fleet in the middle of Never-Never land.

One boat stocked his bilge with wine from Australia and to keep the bottles from clinking he filled the spaces in between with golf balls. When the wine was gone, he donated the balls and a 3 iron to the cause at a party just before he left westbound. We hit the balls as hard as we could out into the lagoon and then swam around collecting them, just to do it again. Chagos was so great.

We had kite flying days. We had Mexican night pot luck where Karen made tortillas from scratch and cooked them up on the beach. We had Hawaiian night and 'funny hat made out of coconut fronds' night. There were always boats coming and leaving, all which required a party. Once the British destroyer, which hung around to keep fishing boats away and to collect our fees, came in and held a British barbeque on the beach which was fun after we got used to drinking gin while eating stuffed pig. Again the days ran together till it was like a long summer vacation that never ended. But it did end. Chagos was so great. Too bad it had to end. I had a decision to make. Too bad I made the wrong one.

What we should have done when the time was right was to head west towards South Africa, turn the corner and go up the Atlantic back to America. Falcon had just turned 13 and we were wondering what to do about High School. The question was should we continue our lotus eating life style or head back to America. It was unfair to ask Karen or Falcon as they both would have replied, Calvin like, 'Is this a trick question?' Finally after much soul searching and discussing it with my fellow Captains I decided to return to Thailand for the Southwest Monsoon hurricane season and then in winter we would give Chagos another go and then continue west about. It was a popular decision but I wasn't sure it was a proper one. We had a good trip up to the Maldives to pick up some fresh food. (Again we didn't leave Chagos till we had nothing, and I mean nothing, left to eat on the boat. And after 5 months we were ready for civilization again) There was a bit of weather in the Bay of Bengal but it was forecast to dissipate.

It didn't. It intensified, dramatically. After two days we were in some of the roughest squalls I have ever been in. It was reef the sails, shake them out, reef 'em, shake 'em, endlessly day after day. On the fifth day we were still only 400 miles out from Addu and were taking a beating. That's when the killer whales showed up. I had been rammed by whales before; no, that's not true, I did the ramming.

I was on Time Out in the middle of the Indian Ocean. It was one of those perfect days you only get in the Indian. Everyone was sleeping under the noon sun. The birds were sitting on the water sleeping. The fish snoozed as my lure passed in front of their noses. I dosed in the cockpit. A sperm whale slept dead ahead on the surface. Bang! It was a good thing I was only going 2 knots! The poor whale circled around Time Out, blowing his spout every 5 seconds and staring angrily out of one eye. I jumped up on the rail and said 'I'm sorry' every way I could, accompanied with lots of hand waving. After angrily circling the boat half a dozen times the whale swam off in disgust.

This time it wasn't so pleasant. This time it wasn't calm. This time it was as rough as hell. I must have hit one of the youngsters as in unison the big males hit Beau starboard and port together. How the boat shook! Luckily after teaching us our lesson they left. On diving down later to inspect the damage we were amazed what a few angry whales could do. The hull was bashed in big dents. Later in South Africa we glassed in the hollows and made her stronger than ever. I really thought we could push the hull back into shape once she was out of the water but no; the dents were there to stay. Meanwhile back in the Bay of Bengal we had been talking to a friend four days ahead of us and he was getting bashed about in the bad weather worse than we were. After our little whale attack, I started having second thoughts. Was this a sign that we should be going back to civilization now? Were
we being selfish in returning to Asia for another year? Finally I said, "This is it. We are going back." Falcon was heart broken. He pointed to a tiny little area of blue sky ahead of us.

"Look, Dad, its getting better! Let's keep going." He loved Chagos so much. So back we went to Gan in the

Maldives, a quick stop in Chagos, just to say good bye, and then back to the Seychelles.

I have to hand it to those two. They perked right up after their disappointment and got back into the swing of things. The thing was they really liked the sailing, the freedom to choose where in the world they wanted to go next. Or, I guess, in this case, have me choose for them.

I wasn't too sad about heading back to the US. My biggest worry was that if Falcon didn't circumnavigate with us, he would feel he had to circle the globe on a small boat on his own. Not that it is a bad life; but he should pick it himself, for himself, not because of history. I could just see the future when people found out he had sailed a bit, they would ask,

"What, are you one of those guys who sailed around the world?" If he had to say no, he might feel he had to complete what we didn't do for him. Well, that wasn't going to happen on my watch. And that's a big period, as Karen would say.

One of the tricks of a cruising life style was changing money. Sure, the banks offer the authorized rate. Often a crafty sailor could get a better rate by straying, just a bit, to the wrong side of the law. We wanted to go and visit my Mother in California this coming Christmas (she had organized a freshman year in High School's textbooks) but the tickets from East Africa were very, very expensive. However we could get more than twice the going exchange rate on the black market in the Seychelles. We traded our money, booked the tickets, gave back the Seychelles to Nairobi section of the ticket to the travel agent (part of the slightly illegal deal) and ended up buying return tickets to San Diego from Kenya, for $1500 American for three people!

From the Seychelles we went directly to Kilifi in Kenya where we were to leave the boat for Christmas. Just as we arrived the attack on the World Trade Center on 9/11 took place, and here we were in a predominantly Arab section of Kenya! There was no need to have worried. Arabs from all walks of life came up to us to apologize and to be sure that we knew not all Arabs were terrorists. We watched the news of the initial attack in a food court on a giant TV screen in Mombasa, an Arab city. Arabs around us were weeping as people leaped from the buildings, as they ran panic stricken down streets, as they watched brave firemen running into the buildings to their deaths. They cried openly as the death toll mounted. They asked me what the United States would do, as if I would somehow know. I just replied with an old African saying,

"Never wake a sleeping lion."

Soon we were heading south towards South Africa visiting all the little towns of Kenya, Tanzania and Mozambique. Some areas were rough where we had to guard our boat with a 24 hour watch. Others were fabulous Edens waiting for a boat with more time, to do them justice; to explore their delights.

It was on Isla Mozambique that disaster struck, yet again. Why did this always happen to us? Why couldn't we have nice non-eventful passages? What did I do to get on the universe's bad side? Or is that a trick question?

Isla Mozambique is one of the most unique islands in the Indian. It was one of the main posts of the pre-Columbus and Portuguese exploration of Africa. Even though it is small there are over 600 identified wrecks off the island, dated from before 1800, 12 of them from before 1500. The streets are filled with priceless shards from Chinese tea sets that were washed up from wrecks. Small boys sell necklaces of the original trade beads used by explorers in the 1400's. I bought a bronze and pewter tumbler that belongs in the Smithsonian for three dollars. I keep my pencils in it. The island was a treasure hunter's paradise.

Everything was fine till we tried to leave. Our fresh water pump for the diesel gave up the ghost. The bearings were gone. As nice as Isla Mozambique was it was not a place to fix a diesel. They spoke Portuguese thereabouts which was far from horizontal Spanish, my only foreign language. I found a retired Aid worker from Finland living there. She had worked as a nurse during the 20 year civil war Mozambique had just gone through and had put so much of her life into the country that it was now home. She helped me with translations as I tried to get the black beast fixed. I met a local sport fisherman who drove me inland to the biggest town around. There with his help, the local mechanics made a new set of bearings by hand as nothing they had would fit. In the Western world, mechanics would just throw up their hands and say, 'Can't help you, buddy, it's not in the computer.' And yet we have the nerve to call ourselves the first world. In the back of beyond, they work like the Wright or Ford brothers.

Back on the boat the pump fit and worked beautifully. And then I made a mistake. Potentially a big one. Our translator was watching a friend's Jack Russell for a few months not knowing that the dog was pregnant. Suddenly she was the caretaker of 5 puppies and the owner was incognito. One of the puppies had one regular brown eye and one perfectly formed blue eye. The local fishermen were sure this puppy was an evil spirit and wanted to kill it in a pagan ceremony, complete with pulling the still beating heart out of the living puppy. It was bringing bad luck to the fishing grounds with its evil eye, our friend was told. She asked me if I would take the puppy to the mainland where at least the dog would have a chance to live. The last thing she wanted was to see her little puppy tortured to death just yards from her house. I went and got Karen. She went and got Falcon. Suddenly things were out of my control and we were dog owners. And I had no one to blame except myself.

It soon became apparent that blame was not the correct word. A far better word is brilliance. Yes, I am brilliant. You can say it. Let's hear you say it now. What? Louder. Can't hear you from here! That's better!

Falcon blossomed. Whether it was the responsibility of a dog, something to do with an endless amount of puppy love or it was his time to shine, it is hard to say, but he grew into the boy he was meant to be. But it is not my story. Here is an article Falcon wrote for a good friend and laughing fellow rover, Diane Jesse, author of 'Cruising With Your Four Footed Friends' published by Seaworthy Publications, Inc. and reprinted here with permission.

"I've lived all my life without a family dog but I've always been in contact with them. When I was young, I thought I was good with dogs (what kid doesn't). Then life went on and I gave away all my toys, play guns, and recently most of my precious buddies (stuffed animals). There was no better time for me to find a dog. I was feeling the empty space between childhood and adolescence.

"Dad found Ilia in a nice little water front house in Ilia Mozambique living with a pleasant Finnish retired Aid worker, now self employed. Ilia had a family of seven dogs (all Jack Russell's) including her mother and her brother from another litter. We received Ilia when she was 7 weeks old and brought her into our home and family.

"At this point, I would like to describe our cockpit. It is located in the center of the boat and has two levels one for sitting on and the other for your feet (where the drainage holes are). The second layer at that time in Ilia's life was too tall for her to climb out. As a result we used the bottom layer as a cage without bars.

"I made a cardboard/plastic box house (which she destroyed trying to get out to see us) and a plastic vegetable container with three-quarters of the open part covered by cardboard all equipped with blankets and cushions. In short, she lived like a queen.

"The bottom of the cockpit was her domain for about a month. She had her bed, water, food, hunting territory if you will, and a pee/poop paper (which within a few days changed into a rug, which we later dragged over board when it becomes soiled). She was content, safe, and secure.

"If you are bringing up a dog or are thinking about getting one I would suggest you do intentionally what we did by chance (that being putting her inside a controlled environment, like the lower part of the cockpit).

"We sailed from Ilia Mozambique (where we got the dog, fitting isn't it?) to Bazaruto where she had her first encounter with water, real beaches and walks around islands. One time we walked around the island of Santa Carolina and towards the end of our exhausting trek she had had enough. So I very easily put her in a basket under my shoulder, and she slept the rest of the way. It amazes me how Ilia can sleep anywhere.

"From there we came to Richard's Bay where we are now.

"I would like to express the psychological side of having a dog in two parts the first part labeled BD and the second DD.

"Basic psychology: the grass is always greener on the other side. BD, or before dog, I always wanted a dog, although after I thought about the realities for a while I didn't want to clean up after it, walk, bathe, and be harsh to it when the dog deserved it. At that time the work of caring for a dog was too overpowering for me. So we didn't get a dog by normal means e.g. going to the pound or looking in the paper.

"Instead we found our puppy by chance. (They were going to sacrifice her in a pagan ritual as she has one blue and one brown eye.)

"BD, I wasn't a very kid oriented person; I preferred adult conversations and debates. At that time, I liked grown-ups better because they did not gang up, tease and challenge as many children do. Also I was too eager to grow up (I hadn't read Peter Pan yet) and be respected by grown ups although (in my mind) I was already as experienced, well spoken (I mean vocabulary not speech, I had a small stutter) and as learned as some of them. But after BD was over and the second phase began, I too started a new chapter in my life, DD- during dog.

"I was for once able to play with a living creature that had the same amount of energy as I. I was able to play free from worry of teasing and tension. Able to play, as any kid should be allowed to do. I now have a best friend that I didn't have to sail away from when the boat moved on.

"Now that we are again in society, I find the magic of a longstanding friend to be holding out against all the sieges of social torment. I feel that if a person is lonely or wishing for something more, something much greater than him or herself, that person need not look too far. For a friend will be found in every loved dog, one that will not tease or cause anger, only one that will help when help is needed and love throughout its entire life.

"Although boats are different, we feed Ilia the same way many other people do, with dog pellets, table scraps, bones, and the odd fishtail if we can catch one!

"She now sleeps either on the couch, my bed, my parent's bed, or in her own bed, which she loves dearly. I am very glad we have a Jack Russell, even though they are renowned for their hyperactivity, in no way do they (at least Ilia doesn't) need the same amount of exercise. If we play for about ten minutes 5 times a day with 'rat' (an old sock) and take her for two big walks and maybe one small one she'll be content. When we are sailing, Ilia is at her peak of her happiness, prancing up and down the deck like Captain Bligh, she even loves being at sea more than at anchor. A born sailor if I say so myself, never gotten seasick even once.

"I wish you could see Ilia's little head peeking over the coaming as we row about in the dinghy, grinning in utter happiness. I truly believe that dogs are one of man's best friends. And a boat is a dog's dream come true.

Falcon Riley. Age 14

We were surprised to find Jack Russells in Africa and even more surprised to discover that the Africans used them to hunt lions. They released a pack of them whenever a man-eater stalked a village. Apparently there is no other dog breed that is quick enough, smart enough, and egotistical enough to believe they won't be killed, and also so intensely annoying enough to distract the lion which lets the spearmen get close enough to make the kill. If one or two dogs get killed, that is sad, but their job is to protect the village.

Soon we were in Richard's Bay, South Africa. It was winter down by the Cape of Good Hope, definitely not a good time to sail with our little toy sailboat. We had to wait for spring, 5 months away. Luckily, South Africa had just devalued the Rand and life for us was very cheap. We ate like kings and stayed at a slip in a marina! Falcon bought himself a Hobie 14 for $200 American and had a great time sailing it behind the sand bars in flat water when the Southerly Busters blew in with 50 knots plus!

At night after dinner we would watch a movie and were puzzled at Falcon's questions. He would ask the most fundamental questions about why the hero was doing this or that. Finally it dawned on us that he couldn't see the actor's faces well enough to understand their motivation. We took him to the clinic and soon he had his own pair of glasses. Suddenly he started to laugh at the right places in the movie!

Karen didn't have to watch her pocketbook as everything was so cheap, but old lessons are not easily forgotten. Falcon was just as bad. Every price had to be evaluated in terms of value and quality for the buck. The two of them would spend hours in the grocery store buying just a few items. That's not fair. I was worse!

We had a Zulu local sand the interior of the whole boat which I then painted. He was very reasonably priced. We gave him a bit extra as he was a college student saving up for his next semester. We went on more Safaris and took hikes up into the mountains. What a truly lovely country. A friend left his car in Richard's Bay while he sailed half the way to Cape Town. He left the keys for us to deliver his car to him. He was in no hurry and we took the opportunity to explore the interior of the country.

Falcon decided he would rather stay on the boat. He wanted some alone time. We thought, discussed and debated if he could be left alone at the grand old age of 14. Normally the answer would be no, no, no. Falcon, however, was very mature for his age and he lived in a marina full of friends. We organized for him to have dinner on a different boat each night while we were gone. (He ended up inviting whoever he was supposed to eat with to Beau Soleil where he cooked them dinner!) He had his school work to do and Ilia to keep him company. Karen worried a bit in the way of mothers, but I remembered how wild and capable I was at 14 and had no worries about the ever so competent Falcon.

Soon it was time to leave, to head south. This was the area where 100 foot plus waves, which easily sank huge ships, lurked. Massive lows marched across the Southern Ocean and dominated the weather patterns. They surged between the tip of Africa and Antarctica to the south accelerating to get through to the open waters of the Indian beyond. My old nemesis, the Agulhas current attained rates of 5 to 8 knots off the coast, luckily in the direction we wanted to go. But unlucky too; if we got caught out at sea when a southerly buster slammed against the contrary current it would create waves that could easily sink the boat. We had to be sure that the 'window' we choose to leave in would last long enough to see us into port. The first step was the longest, 500 plus miles and the windows often only lasted 2 to 3 days. On that trip Falcon, always a lover of more sail, managed to fly 11 sails, all drawing at the same time! It was a good thing we were making 10 to 12 knots!

Each port we stopped in was unique in its own right. In East London the free dock had a road that led up to the main street that was lined with a 15 foot stone wall on each side. Falcon took it into his head that he was a rock climber and he spent hours each day transversing the wall, end to end, as cars zoomed below him. It drove his mother crazy. She was sure that he was going to fall and kill himself and wondered why he was doing something so stupid. I had to remind her that it was no good complaining that after leading your mule to water, he drank.

"We've spent our whole lives espousing independence and self determination, should we be surprised when those qualities show up in our own child?"

At sea, we raced down huge waves. We competed who could surf Beau the fastest. Falcon won with a speed of 17.8 knots and that was while we were towing a 100 yards of warps.

He rocked climbed all along the South African coast. He was in seventh heaven when we climbed Table Mountain in Cape Town. Even when we got caught in a lightning storm atop the mountain, he loved it. He loved it even when a lightning bolt hit 20 yards away. Granted, his mother was a lot closer to the strike than he, she was within 20 feet, but he still loved the experience. Karen insisted on gathering her flowers under the lightning, storm or no storm. Even when the soles of her tennis shoes melted from the lightning, she wouldn't stop gathering her wild flowers. Why was she surprised in her son's behavior? In Simon's Town, where we stopped for a while, he organized all his friends into a climbing club and they spent the afternoons after school on the rocks. On rainy days they stayed in the gym and did endless one handed pull ups.

Soon we were off to the north where we called in at Namibia. Luderitz is the place where diamonds are found laying around on the beach.   We tried to walk the dog on the beach, but someone must have tried that already. They didn't fall for it. We were escorted back to the boat. The streets were lined with very high quality quartz which Karen was positive had diamonds embedded inside. Every time we went to the grocery store she came back with one bag of groceries and one of quartz. As the waterline went down, I started to secretly dump the quartz back into the street at night as she had filled every locker she could.

We spent a slow two weeks drifting towards St. Helena, an island in the middle of the South Atlantic most famous as the island Napoleon was exiled to after he escaped from Elba when the British didn't hold up their end of the surrender agreement. Falcon, more and more a history buff, loved it. We learned more in a week about Napoleon's last days and death than anyone but a college professor had any right to know. The best part of the island was the landing. The surge was so bad in the island's only anchorage that as the dinghy came into the cement pier we leapt for overhanging lines and Tarzan like swung onto the dock with the dinghies' painter in our teeth. The first time was very scary but after a week, we acted like old hands. The
coast of the island was a series of solid cliffs, but the interior could have come from England. It was truly beautiful, with gently rolling hills and crofts here and there for the sheep. Napoleon's house was on top of a hill overlooking a beautiful landscape. The only bad part was the British had painted every wall and floor with paint

laced with arsenic and were slowly poisoning him to death. The whole world was deathly afraid of that one little man.

We had discovered that there was a rally for our type of boat, a Dickerson, in June, on the Eastern Shore of Maryland. We were hard pressed for time to make the rally, so we bypassed Ascension and Brazil and headed directly towards Barbados. It was a spooky passage as the Saharan dust was as thick as fog. Huge ships appeared out of nowhere just a mile from us. The boat was repainted a dusty brown only to return to her normal colors when we reached the trades and rain up at 11° north.

Ilia was quarantined on board both in Barbados and St. Helena. To exercise her we swam around the boat endless times. She spent 50 days aboard till we landed at Martinique. She took it into her head to hate flying fish. Her little doggie ears could hear even the tiniest baby flying fish landing on deck which required barking and growling and much racing around the deck.

In Barbados we anchored out by the reef in a nice little cut and enjoyed exploring the island. One day Falcon tired of our endless circles (our lives seem bound by circles, according to Falcon, everything we do, we end up back where we started; shopping, sailing, cooking, living) so he choose to stay on the boat. Good thing, too. While we were gone, our anchor started to drag and soon the boat was only 5 feet from the coral. Fourteen year old Falcon raised the 265 pounds of anchor and chain, hand over hand, by himself, started the boat, found a better spot and reanchored perfectly. If there was going to be a graduation exercise for cruising, he just passed with flying colors. The local men (who were getting ready for a bit of salvage) complimented him profusely.

After quick stops in Martinique, Puerto Rico, the Dominican Republic, Turks and Caicos, and the Bahamas, we were off towards Beaufort in North Carolina. After a long day of riding, the horse (Beau) could smell her stable and she picked up her pace. We tried to slow down, especially in the Abacos as we knew that we were to be embayed for the next three years. We were going to give Falcon a taste of a 'normal' education. It wasn't fair to release him into the world and out of our care when he went to college with an unrealistic view of the day to day operation of the world. Most people live lives of 'quiet desperation'. Most people don't spend their lives wandering the world doing pretty much whatever they please when ever they wanted to do it. How would this child of the sea and of freedom react to the captivity of High School in Annapolis? It would be interesting to find out; or rather not find out, as disaster again lay lurking ahead.

Karen of ~~Troy~~ The Seven Seas

STARTING TO SOLO

I used to like Annapolis. It was a real cruising town. If you anchored too close to the channel or even in it, no one cared. A cop didn't come out at midnight and rouse you to make you move like in Florida. There are many free dinghy tie ups, with ladders made of stainless, all with garbage facilities. There are scores of jobs for 'itinerant' workers, especially those who have their own floating housing.

I didn't know about Annapolis's dark evil secret then. I didn't know about the snake in this Eden. I didn't know about the school board. But I found out.

We happily walked into the local high school to enroll Falcon for the upcoming school year. I smiled at everyone glad to be starting a new phase of Falcon's education. The principal didn't smile back.

"Where did the boy attend grade school?"

"He was home schooled while sailing around the world." I thought I had just said the magic words to open doors in Annapolis. The principal just sniffed.

"How old is the boy?"

"He is l4 as he completed two grades in one year," I explained proudly.

"All l4 year olds are freshmen."

"Falcon has already finished his freshman year with flying colors."

"All l4 year olds are freshmen." There was no change in her expression.

"If you don't believe me, just test him."

"We don't do that."

"What?"

"All l4 year olds are freshmen."

We talked to the school district's superintendent and got the same answer. All three of us were trained by the sea and when faced with adversity and heavy squalls, we were used to hunkering down and trying a little harder. But we really didn't expect to find such a totalitarian stonewall in the land of the free.

We went to other school districts in the area.

"If he is l4 then he is a freshman." Every time we said, just test him, we were told,

"We don't do that."

Did we make a major mistake in home schooling our child? Should have we returned him to formal schooling earlier? Or were we just observing a major negative reaction to the growing popularity of home schooling in the United States? If Falcon had to repeat his freshman year it would destroy formal education for him. He knew the work so well he would coast and get into trouble out of boredom. And in any city, anywhere in the world, trouble is not hard to find if you are looking for it.

To take our minds off our predicament we sailed over towards the rural Eastern Shore of Maryland to join in with the rest of our type of sailboats, built by Dickerson, for a race and a rally in Oxford, Maryland. The winner of the race gets to be Commodore for the next year. Falcon was sure we were going to win. He was used to his lockers being filled to the brim with food. He was used to being gentle with our old worn out sails. But he needed some cheering up after the disappointments of the last week. We did alright, finished in the middle of the pack after we fell into a hole with no wind. But the party was great and the people were laughing fellow rovers and you can't ask for better than that.

While we were there in Oxford, we thumbed a ride up to the high school in Easton, 11 miles away. We explained our situation, I didn't do a lot of smiling, and I was smiled out. The principal looked us up and down and said,

"I don't know. Home schooled on a boat. Fourteen years of age. I'm sorry, but we will have to test him."

Yes! Finally! Hurrah! But. To qualify for that school district we had to reside within it. We sailed back to Annapolis where our good friends from the Pacific, the 'Jump Up's' had lent us a dock for the summer. We hopped into our $1000 rolling wreck of a car and zoomed back to Easton. To enroll Falcon we needed a local address.

We resumed our habit of looking for hurricane holes or in this case winter storm holes. We drove down every road we could find looking for people with docks that they were willing to rent. Eventually we found a bulkhead, with 12 feet of water under it (extremely deep for the Chesapeake), owned by two businessmen who hoped to one day turn it into a marina. They were kind enough to rent us part of their bulkhead for a nominal cost. We had an address to sign up Falcon to go to school! The school board gave Falcon the final exams for the freshman year in World

History, English, Earth Science and Math all of which he aced with 92 percent or better with no cramming, taking it cold and with his parents rushing around like their heads were cut off.

The school and the area were rural. Our dock was just at the edge of the city limits. It was 2 miles to the high school; 1 mile to the YMCA; a 20 minute walk to the closest grocery store and the library.

Easton was the county seat and was the center of shopping. Our dock was on Port Street, which we were told, was definitely on the wrong side of the tracks. We didn't know, after so long in Africa we found black faces normal. Teachers at Falcon's school were aghast that one of their white students was living in danger. Falcon just laughed at them. He was to receive an education in more than just the three R's in the next three years. And the school would have their eyes opened, too. Falcon's answers came from a different slant than most, naturally, considering how he spent his past years of schooling.

I didn't have any trouble living on Port Street. Sure there were shootings and robberies. That didn't have anything to do with me. Most radical parts of the world operate on the pay back system. When one person or group does something 'bad' to another, the do-it-to-ers then become the been-done-ers. As long as we could avoid giving offense to anyone we would be safe. I didn't allow Karen to walk down the street by herself. With me, she was fine. After awhile we became part of the street, we were the people who lived on that boat with the dog. Ilia was a favorite with the whores and the drug dealers on the corners. The first wanted to pet her and give her treats; the second wanted to buy her as a guard dog.

It didn't take long till we were employed. First we worked for our old friends Diane and Jim Jesse who had sold their sailboat, swallowed the sheets and bought a motorboat in the next town up the road. It was a woody and needed a lot of work. After that, we took odd jobs. Karen worked as a substitute at the local schools. The State school board stated (actually they hissed) that they wouldn't recognize her East Coast credentials. She wasn't too unhappy. Working as a substitute gave her much more free time to spend with her son.

On one odd job, I delivered phone books during the first snow storm of the year. I didn't dress properly (not knowing any better) and eventually the cold made me want to pee in the worse way. I squeezed a certain part of my anatomy as I rushed into a restaurant's facility. I didn't realize, through my gloves, that I was frozen solid. I broke some blood vessels inside of me and bled like a woman for three days. Karen and Falcon were freaked and wanted me to go to the hospital but the blood was bright red so I wasn't worried that it was serious. It stopped after a bit. Anyway what would have a doctor done? Cut me open? Yeah, right.

Eventually Karen worked in a marine store (she felt if you are building a house, work in a lumber yard; if you are fixing up an old boat, work in a marine store). I drove a nine car ferry from Oxford over to a landing by St. Michaels. Falcon became a life guard at the YMCA and donated some of his time to get service hours, a requirement for graduation.

We soon settled in. The library had a good selection of DVD's for no charge. We still were following our life at sea by keeping our expenses at a minimum. We had been doing it for so long we couldn't see our way to act any differently. There was a charity on our street that got supermarkets to donate day old bread which they then left on a table by the parking lot for hungry people. That included us! Falcon was now a major eater. He usually ate three or four sandwiches on arriving home and then asked what was for dinner. Karen liked the bread table as the locals took all the white and left the multigrain, European, rye, and other more exotic breads for bird feed. There were 5 different supermarkets in town and we developed the habit of buying only what was on sale. The only problem was winter was definitely here. Our tropical blood was experiencing a different way of life.

I hadn't been in snow since 5th grade. Falcon never had. He had never built a snowman or had a snowball fight. Karen, who grew up in Connecticut, filled our ears with stories about winter. We believed every tale. Falcon couldn't wait. I spent every spare hour winterizing the boat. Good thing I did too!

Initially Falcon loved school. Back in Malaysia when we were buying pirated CD's for Falcon's school work, we also bought many teenage movies. Finally Falcon was acting in his own high school movie. He was delighted. Until he started to realize how curt, uncaring, rude and dysfunctional people could be. Through all his school years, Falcon was a star. He was our star during home schooling. He was a star in first grade for taking on the upperclassmen. He was a star in the Seychelles for having come from so far away. He was a star in Chagos for taking on a tiger shark and walking away. He was a star in South Africa because of his rock climbing exploits. He never let his 'stardom' go to his head. He always stood up for the little guy. If there was one kid in an anchorage that had no one to play with, Falcon would make time to hang out with him. This attitude didn't work well in Easton High. There was a mix of students; rich farmer kids, 'white trash' (hey, that's what they called themselves!), poor blacks, rich blacks, Asians, and Hispanics. Easton was such a rural society that all the students had known each other since first grade. Where was Falcon going to fit in?

Soon we noted a lack of enthusiasm for school. He grew up on the boat in a very polite society. There you couldn't afford to make enemies. If you got into trouble; broken engine, hard aground on the reef, busted mast, the boat you had offended might be the only one near enough that could help you. You had to be polite. Well, most of us did. Karen insisted on calling an ace an ace, no matter what. She wasn't one to pull punches, especially when it came to not standing watches.

Some boats bragged that they slept thru the night at sea; they stood no watch at night, they slept the night through. When Karen met them socially she refused to shake their hands. She glared at them and said,

"I don't want to get to know dead people. I might start to like you then I'll have to cry when you don't turn up after a passage. Don't talk to me. You're just so much dead meat. Go away." Karen would travel to the ends of the earth for her friends. Even for perfect strangers she would go to great lengths to help them out. Just don't get her blood up! Anyway back to Easton, Maryland.

Falcon couldn't understand why kids were so mean to each other. I couldn't help him. I told him that this is the way the world works. The way he grew up was exceptional. Most people are so unhappy they take it out on others. I told him to get used to it. I told him that there are two ways to feel good about oneself. One is to go out and bust your butt to accomplish whatever strikes your fancy. The other is to tear everyone else down by belittling them to make yourself feel like you are the better man. The first is a matter of guts and determination. The second is the creed of the second-hander. (Thanks, Ayn) This one's success exists only in the failure of others. He lives his life only as a reflection in the eyes of others. I asked Falcon to decide what kind of man he was going to be. I told him, I didn't want an answer. I told him to decide by himself for himself.

Everyday it got colder. Some nights it fell to minus temperatures. And everyday I added more and more insulation. I bought sheets of R-3 and cut them to shape to fit between the deck beams and the ceiling frames in

Falcon's forepeak. (For some unknown reason, ceilings on a boat are on the sides not the overhead. I really think that all these nautical terms are just to keep landlubbers in the dark until they pay up for their passage!) I added insulation under all the settees and berths. Along the hull, I layered aluminum foil with bubble wrap. Part of the problem with our bulkhead dock that first winter, was we only had a 15 amp extension cord for power. We could only run two little electric space heaters for warmth. I didn't mind. Karen cuddled me all night long. Forget the tropics! Give me a cold winter and a hot dame any time!

Driving in the snow was new to me. Our boat was close to Easton's only boat launching ramp so the snow plows kept our street clear. The trouble was stopping. My first experience was very frightening. It was like being broached by the big greybeards down in the roaring forties. As I approached a light, during the first snow of the season and braked the car, it somehow turned in slow circles, still sliding towards the red light! I had to hand it to the East coast drivers. The cars who now had a green light sat there dead in the water as my car twirled through the intersection. Somehow in ended up on the other side in the right lane and facing the correct way! It does help to be lucky in life!

Sailing is all about keeping your vessel under control; reefing early, maintaining steerageway in harbors, towing warps in big breaking seas. (We have two dedicated self tailing winches on Beau just for controlling warps, one on each side of the stern cabin. With a little practice it is easy to put the blight of the warp just at the spot, usually two or three boat lengths back, where the waves start to curl and break. The warp messes with the water enough to keep the wave from breaking on top of the boat.) Sailing is all about control. Imagine my unhappiness sliding sideways towards a red light, totally out of control. The car stopped in time, thanks St. Jude! Thank goodness the patron saint of hopeless cases and sailors is effective on shore as well as at sea!

Falcon was very interested in all of this and in anything automotive. In Maryland teens could start their driver training at 15¾ years of age, one year from now! I should start driving better to give him a good example! He traded some hours of work with one of our bulkhead owners for a racing bike. He thought it was beneath him to be driven to school by his parents, and especially to be picked up at the end of the day. When we did come to pick him up on rainy and snowy days we had to wait a block away, never in front of the school. On weekends we would take him to vacant parking lots to practice his driving skills. Unfortunately or fortunately, our car was a manual and Falcon was having a great deal of trouble coordinating hand and foot at
the same time, but eventually he got it. My nerves survived about as well as the clutch plate.

Maryland was very strict on the procedures for new drivers. They had to go to driver education. They couldn't have passengers other than adults for the first year. After that they could only have one passenger at a time for six months. Any moving violation sent the clock back to zero. Falcon wanted to practice with us till he was very sure of himself; not that he wasn't a good driver. He was. After all, he had driven down 90 Mile Beach in New Zealand as practice!

After our Dickerson rally we, and 2 other Dickerson 41s sister ships, stopped at a dock and beautiful property that belonged to an ex-Dickerson owner. Falcon got the job of driving the sit-on mower for hours a day. He loved it and hardly ever hit trees or ran over flowers!

Karen was still substituting for the school system at this time and was very careful to ask Falcon each time she was offered a job at the high school if it would be OK with him if she worked there. He always said yes. These school kids couldn't believe that 5' 6" Karen had swam with and dominated sharks. It was weird, kind of. Here was this little normal looking (with exciting moments of pure beauty) girl, who could be and was your next door neighbor, and she had done all these unusual things. How could they be blamed for doubting? None of us pushed it. I have always been leery of fame. Fame has ruined many a good man. Besides if everyone knows what you are doing, someone for sure is going to come up and tell you to stop it. Most likely, Big Brother!

After school Falcon and I would throw the old pigskin or a Frisbee around on the gravel parking lot in front of the boat. Ilia thought it was her game and would race from person to person. When we missed the football Ilia would be after it in a flash. All she could grab was the laces but it was tough to get it back from her. She had been sitting on the boat all day and had energy to burn. She loved going on walks especially with Falcon. After my 'fun is as important as school, home schooling program' on the boat, real life was coming on hard and fast. But he didn't want to talk about it. He considered school as his own personal battle and didn't want to share it whether it was a victory or a defeat. He kept his school life separate. On parent teacher nights, everyone was full of compliments. He made good grades, not great but good. I was sure he was spending most of his time experimenting with or developing, a working theory about cliques and friendships. That's what really interested him. We told him he had to start thinking about college but our words didn't translate.

Soon summer arrived. Falcon still was a rabid rock climber so we sent him off to a 10 day climbing camp in Colorado. We arranged, that after the camp, he flew on to spend a month in Coronado with my mother. It was the first time he had flown alone. Here was this kid who had sailed around the world but always had his parents by his side. Maybe I see why Falcon wanted to keep part of his life for himself.

The hot sticky summer was soon over. I had broken down and installed an air conditioner in a hatch just to insure survival. Boil in the summer, freeze in the winter, and people spend their whole lives like this? Don't they know they are supposed to cross the equator in the summer to stay away from the heat and the hurricanes?

His Junior Year started with a bang. He joined the debate team and after the first week he returned from school and told me that I had wasted my life running away from responsibility. There were many ways to answer that question, but I picked the most debate friendly.

"Running from is a negative thing. I don't do negative. Never have. I have spent my life running towards life. When I see a better, happier way to live, I run that way. My life is based on the pursuit of happiness, not on reacting to fear. Running from is a fear thing. Besides, running from entails turning your back and I have never been good at that. I'm much better at running towards the responsibility of making my life and the lifes of those around me, happier."

Falcon had figured out school now and he started joining sports teams. He signed up for the swimming team. The coach asked me where he had swum before. I told him this was his first team. We both turned and watched Falcon surge up and down the pool. He had a hell of a bow wave flowing down his sides. I could feel the coach's disbelief.

"Well, he has spent quite a few years spear fishing around the world." The coach looked at me in surprise and then nodded. Mostly, in a competitive school like Easton, beginning swimmers never make the varsity. Falcon took third in State in the l00 yard butterfly.

He joined the cross country team. Like most sailors, he wasn't a natural runner but he had heart. He hurt his leg in the first race of the season but he wouldn't quit. It was painful to watch him run. It was more of a fast hobble than a run. Karen and I tried to talk him into quitting, he wouldn't.

When he went to the grocery store with us after school, my heart ached. Not for Falcon, for my own lost youth. Every teenage girl we passed would go,

"Hiiiiii, Falcon," with lots of fluttering eyelashes. He would grunt,

"Hi," as he walked on by. My goodness, what a swath he could have carved! But on the other hand it wasn't much more than a year ago that he was in Africa where entire villages were decimated from HIV. Grandmothers had 20 grandchildren to care for with no income, as all their own children were dead. Hundreds of people walked by on the street as thin as rails, just waiting to die. No wonder he was put off dating. But still! Wow!

One day, riding his bike home from school on the 'by-pass', a 50 mph road, Falcon's front wheel came off. He liked driving very fast, getting his exercise in, but as I always told him, speed kills. Luckily he landed on his backpack full of school books, his head just inches from the traffic. Considering the speed he was going he wasn't too badly scared up. In Malaysia we had taken him ice skating at a shopping mall and he had fallen and banged his head on the ice; afterwards, he complained of reoccurring headaches. The only good part of his bicycle accident was his headaches finally went away. Hey, maybe that Chinese doctor in Malaysia that wanted to break Karen's foot the other way was right!

Falcon discovered Advance Placement Classes. These are more difficult classes covering high school subjects at the college level. Upon completion of a national test at the end of the class, college credit was given. Falcon started taking nothing but AP classes. He seemed to like the challenge and the better quality of classmates such classes generated. By the end of high school he had earned a year's worth of college credit!

Falcon got his Learners Permit and our nerves were tested again. It was a very good thing we lived in the country where there wasn't a lot of traffic. He needed plenty of room! It's also a good thing that our nerves had been tested by countless squalls and survived, twanged but intact.

Falcon's teeth had started out fairly straight but as he grew his body didn't keep up with the size of his teeth. One of the things we wanted to accomplish during the high school years was to get them straightened. The orthodontists we went to on the Eastern Shore were of the old school.

"We'll just pull these four teeth to give the others room to grow." It wasn't like these were cavity ridden, rotten teeth. They were perfect in every way. It took six months of searching, but finally were found an orthodontist who said,

"What do you want to pull teeth for? We'll straighten all of them." He was expensive, but what the hell, we were working and he was our only kid.

The next summer Falcon returned to climbing camp in Colorado and hence on to Coronado but this time for only a couple of weeks. He wanted to return early to Maryland as he wanted to join the football team which required weight training camp during the summer. His mother was freaked.

"We paid all this money to get his teeth straightened and now he is going to go get them all knocked out!" Falcon took his weight training seriously. He was driving himself to school now as he was a full fledged driver. We bought a second car as he seemed to have appropriated our old one. How easily we could get sucked into life ashore. We fought the influence of civilization every minute of every day but still we now had a microwave, a plug in refrigerator, an air conditioner, 3 heaters, a new TV, a DVD player, and plug in fans on board. No doubt the washer and dryer would soon follow!

The price for our bulkhead had slowly risen over the years and it got to the point that it was time to move on. We ended up at a marina down in Oxford next to both the ferry I was driving and the marine store where Karen was working. Falcon had a longer drive to school every day but that was good in a way as it was along a straight two lane country road where the greatest danger was hitting a deer. He was able to improve his driving skills in a relatively safe environment.

On weekends he and his friends went to various rock climbing parks around Maryland. Most of them involved driving on the beltway circling Washington, DC, a road as bad as any in LA. It was dangerous for a new driver, but it was great practice also.

Oxford was a great little town. There were seven marinas in a town of 792 permanent residents. In the summer it was booming, in the winter, when we were there, it was a sleepy little town known mostly because of the ferry, that I was driving, which was the oldest privately owned ferry in the United States. We didn't worry about summer. As soon as Falcon graduated we were off! We were bound for New England and Maine for the summer. We wanted one last cruise as a family before Falcon left to go to college. We wanted our last months together to be spent, as so much of our life had been spent, sailing together.

Falcon qualified for the National Honor Society and was accepted at the University of San Diego (his first choice) and awarded a scholarship of 20,000 dollars for the first year. Falcon then turned them down. The tuition was an additional 15,000 and there was no commitment for a scholarship for the continuing years. We tried to tell him the university just wanted to see how well he did, if he got good grades then he would get more scholarship monies. He was adamant. He decided instead to get his California residency and to attend a Junior College for the upcoming year. We were aghast. This was not what we had planned in our minds. Falcon told us he wasn't interested in our plans. It was his life and he was going to live it his way. Where had all this self determination come from? Would it have been better to have kept him in school for all those years?

We were aghast at first but on further study discovered 2 US Senators and 7 Congressmen had attended Mesa College, Falcon's choice. He felt that he wasn't going to get his money's worth at college, so why not limit his expenditure.

His point was that if it was just a piece of paper; why not spend less for the first two years. The diploma at the end was the same from a big four year school, whether he spent two years there or four. We couldn't complain. We had spent our lives at sea limiting our expenditures and attempting to get the best value for the best price. He felt he was being suckered in with a bait and switch by the University. He was just doing what he was taught by us. As for education, Falcon expected, like in high school, that he would spend more time teaching his classmates about the realities of the planet we all live on than learning from them or his teachers. We tried telling him that college is different. I don't think he believed us. But still $20,000.00!

Falcon came home crushed. They wouldn't let him play football with his glasses on and without them he couldn't see the ball. He was so sad. He had tried so hard to make the team. He put more effort into the swim team instead.

Eventually graduation day came and we were free! It was a big gamble we took, staying still in one place for three years, but we made it without creating irreconcilable differences between the three of us! We were still on our honeymoon!

Down East was great. Being a Californian I had always bad mouthed the East Coast as industrialized, polluted, crowded, and snobby. I had to eat crow. I had such a great time. And Maine! Maine was to die for. If it didn't get so cold in the winter we all would live there. We went all the way north to Machias where my great, great, great grandfather (an O'Brien on my mother's side) had taken part in the first naval action of the Revolutionary War. The British came to town and wanted lumber to build a fort down in Boston. This was just after the Tea Party, and the Colonies were in an uproar. When my fore-bearer refused and raised a liberty pole (like raising a middle finger!), the British stole some lumber and took off running with the Mainers in hot pursuit. The British had a sloop with 14 guns, the Mainers pitchforks and rakes. With their superior sailing skills, the Colonists won the day and took the Brits captive.

We had thought of carrying on to Nova Scotia but we had run out of time. Karen's side of the family was having their bi-yearly get-together and Falcon wanted to go to meet all of his relatives on his mother's side. We hadn't been able to find a mooring safe enough or a marina cheap enough so I had to stay with the boat. Karen and Falcon had great fun planning what they were to take in the car. Those two really liked to pack. Me, I just waited till the last minute and threw stuff in the bag. From the reunion Falcon was to fly directly on to San Diego to start his college career.

My son was leaving. We had lived together in love and admiration and joy for almost every minute of 18 years. Now he was leaving. He was going to leave a big hole in our lives. And, damn, I was going to have to buy an anchor windlass.

I apologize to you, my son, for such a life of adventure. Looking back as I wrote this book I realize I have cursed you, Falcon, with an exceptional life. Because of your childhood, it will be difficult to live a 'normal' life. While others watch movies on TV, you will be replaying home movies in your head. Please Falcon; use your memories not as a goal, but as a trampoline to bounce forward to new exciting moments of your own. Hey, as the prophet said, 'What is past is prologue."

Good bye and good luck, Falcon, my son. And come home, come home soon.

Falcon Fishing in the Seychelles

HIS OWN MAN

Falcon was accepted at the college of his choice. His life was going ahead, full throttle. He was the happiest kid I ever saw. He had a great girl friend, a wonderful job and good prospects. Did anything we do as parents, in bringing him up, help him turn out this way or was it all destiny or good luck? Did our locus eating life style help him or hurt him or didn't it matter in the long run? Did we do anything right or did it all come down to chance?

Did he learn determination and stubbornness of purpose when we pulled our friend's boat 'Gumboot' off the reef in the Tuamotus? Bob and Jenny were ready to give up, ready to abandon the boat. We said 'No Way,' and doubled our efforts to get the boat off the reef. And succeeded.

Did he learn single mindedness when his Mother allowed him to rock climb on cliffs in anchorages around the world? It wasn't easy for her to let him be in danger without her helping hand near. She let him go, knowing that he would fly away, but knowing too, that if she did, he would always fly back.

Did he learn courage staring down sharks on countless reefs throughout the tropics? Staring into the eyes of death of an attacking tiger shark could have paralyzed his personal development for life. Why didn't it? Was it because he had faced lesser challenges before, throughout his life?   Did learning to row the dinghy, mastering the Bermuda sling, learning to windsurf, caring for a pair of sparrows, help?

Did he learn laughter, attending beach parties on beautiful islands?   He grew up with parents who liked to have a good time, who had many friends and made new ones easily.   His lifestyle was such that he made friends within hours of arriving in a new port.   In our lives laughter and parties were reward for a job well done; we took on the sea and somehow managed not to die, we earned our happiness.

Did he learn joy breathing the fabled air of Chagos while standing on his foredeck floating in Never-Never land?   There are places in the world that for one reason or the other exude contentment.   Chagos is one.   Middle Percy on the Reef, Direction Island in Cocos Keeling, Adam's Peak in Sri Lanka are others.   The question of what life is all about could never be asked in places like these.   And having spent time in such a place means that a piece of it will stay in your soul forever.

Did he develop a good work ethic becoming an entrepreneur in harbors around the world?   In every rich country we sailed to we always looked for work.   Whether it was a day's work or a hurricane season's worth, he learned by example that if he wanted work it was there waiting for him.

Did he become a racially mature man by meeting and making friends of people of all colors and types?   In the 58 countries he cruised, in only 5 of them were Caucasians the predominate race.   The people of the world outside America, Europe and the Antipodes are not white.   Falcon learned that from the gut up.

Did he learn love growing up with two people devoted to an everlasting honeymoon?   Our love is not a sugar sweet Pollyanna type of love.   Two head strong individuals like Karen and I are sure to have our differences. The weird part is we are always arguing for what we think the other wants. We each give the other the best and the most of the food. We each let the other sleep and wake on their own time rather than roughly wake them for their watch. And touch! I can't get enough of rubbing her feet; she watches an hour of TV rubbing my back. Karen continually tries to buy me clothes while I endlessly encourage her to buy more sexy bikinis. (Well, maybe that part is for me!) You know, maybe our love is a bit too sugar sweet! I am going to start thinking of me first. Yeah.

Didn't work. I just love that girl too much!

Is education just about school learning? Who is teaching our children how to be adults? The schools sure aren't. I take that back. They are; but our kid's teachers aren't at the blackboard, they are the drug dealers in the playground, and the bullies in the hallways, the sluts in the girl's bathrooms, and boredom on every kid's face in the classrooms.

Does education stop at the doors of the school? Wild animals learn by watching their peers and their parents. How do you think your kids are learning? Are you there for them?

Oh, you are going to send your kid to an expensive private school? Do you think drug dealers don't follow the money? Do you think the bullies don't become verbal; the sluts, self seeking; and the boredom is less because the kids already have it made?

Sorry to tell you this Faithful Reader and Fellow Adventurer, but as always it comes down to you. He is your kid. It really is up to you. It always has been. Let the mask of civilization drop from your eyes, let the animal within climb out and fight for your kid. He is yours; they are trying to take him. Take him back. Do it. Do it now.

In French Polynesia

AFTERWORD

Canned Goods store where we stocked up in San Diego is no longer there.

Rabaul where I met Karen in New Guinea has been destroyed in a massive eruption. No plans are envisioned to rebuild.

The footprint on top of Sri Pada has been covered with cement and a fake footprint put on top as people insisted on putting their own foot into the real footprint to check out the fit, which was considered a sacrilege.

The Gulf of Aden is infested with pirates mostly along the Somalia border. The war lords discovered marine radios and GPS are 12 volt, the same as their jeeps, and are trying to equip their armies. Plus they discovered kidnapping. They roam out as far as the outer banks of the Seychelles.

Port Sudan, where we got the sword, has turned fundamentalist and is now bypassed by almost all cruising boats.

The flower market in Acapulco now covers only a single circus tent.

Chagos now costs $750 for a single month and no extensions or returns allowed.

Gigi, the grey whale we caught, was tracked to Alaska after she was released. There she managed to rid herself of the antenna on her back.

They don't accept coconuts as money in the San Blas Islands anymore. The cruise ships started calling and turned a barter society into a cash based life.

Now most countries charge for entry in one way or another. These days I have to work two months per person per year.

In the South Pacific, French Polynesia food prices are normal if not cheaper than those in islands to the west, until you get to Suva. They are still very inflated compared to Panama or even Mexico.

Other than the above the cruising life is much the same. We stopped in Haiti this year and it could have been like cruising was 30 years ago. We filled the cockpit with veggies and fruits for $20 worth of trading goods. It is a great big adventurous world out there, go grab yourself some!

Circumnavigators—Again!